HUMAN CANNON

by
EDWARD BOND

Methuen New Theatrescripts

*Published in the Royal Court Writers Series
†Published in the RSC Playtexts Series
††Published in the Women's Playhouse Plays Series

SAMBA
by Michael Abbensetts
EAST-WEST & IS UNCLE JACK A CONFORMIST?
by Andrey Amalrik
*BURIED INSIDE EXTRA
by Thomas Babe
*THE LUCKY CHANCE
by Aphra Behn
DEREK & CHORUSES FROM AFTER THE ASSASSINATIONS
HUMAN CANNON
WAR PLAYS
by Edward Bond
SORE THROATS & SONNETS OF LOVE AND OPPOSITION
*THE GENIUS
by Howard Brenton
THIRTEENTH NIGHT & A SHORT SHARP SHOCK!
by Howard Brenton (*A Short Sharp Shock!* written with Tony Howard)
SLEEPING POLICEMEN
by Howard Brenton and Tunde Ikoli
†MOLIÈRE
by Mikhail Bulgakov (in a version by Dusty Hughes)
†MONEY
by Edward Bulwer-Lytton
RETURN TO THE FORBIDDEN PLANET
by Bob Carlton
*THE SEAGULL
by Anton Chekov (in a version by Thomas Kilroy)
FEN
SOFT COPS
by Caryl Churchill
SHONA, LUNCH GIRLS, THE SHELTER
by Tony Craze, Ron Hart, Johnnie Quarrell
WRECKERS
TEENDREAMS
by David Edgar

*MASTERPIECES
by Sarah Daniels
†THE BODY
by Nick Darke
TORCH SONG TRILOGY
by Harvey Fierstein
†OUR FRIENDS IN THE NORTH
by Peter Flannery
*OTHER WORLDS
by Robert Holman
*RAT IN THE SKULL
by Ron Hutchinson
†PEER GYNT
by Henrik Ibsen (translated by David Rudkin)
*INSIGNIFICANCE
CRIES FROM THE MAMMAL HOUSE
by Terry Johnson
FROZEN ASSETS
SUS
BASTARD ANGEL
by Barrie Keeffe
*NOT QUITE JERUSALEM
by Paul Kember
*BORDERLINE
by Hanif Kureishi
TOUCHED
*TIBETAN INROADS
THE RAGGED TROUSERED PHILANTHROPISTS
MOVING PICTURES: Four Plays
(*Moving Pictures; Seachange; Stars; Strive*)
by Stephen Lowe
PROGRESS & HARD FEELINGS
by Doug Lucie
LAVENDER BLUE & NOLI ME TANGERE
by John Mackendrick
THICK AS THIEVES
WELCOME HOME, RASPBERRY, THE LUCKY ONES
by Tony Marchant

HUMAN CANNON

EDWARD BOND

A Methuen New Theatrescript
Methuen · London and New York

For Yvonne Bryceland

A METHUEN PAPERBACK

First published in Great Britain in 1985 as a Methuen Paperback original by Methuen London Ltd, 11 New Fetter Lane, London EC4P 4EE, and in the United States of America by Methuen Inc, 733 Third Avenue, New York, NY 10017.

Copyright © 1985 by Edward Bond

Bond, Edward
    Human cannon.——(A Methuen new theatrescript)
    I. Title
    822'.914   PR6052.05
    ISBN 0 413 57250 1

Printed in Great Britain by Expression Printers Ltd, London N7

CAUTION
This play is fully protected by copyright. All rights are reserved and all enquiries concerning the rights for professional or amateur stage productions should be made to Margaret Ramsay Ltd., 14a Goodwin's Court, St. Martin's Lane, London WC2N 4LL. No performance may be given unless a licence has been obtained.

Spain
The first scene in the late twenties
The other scenes from 1936 to 1940

Part One

1. The Nameless Child — The Ruiz' house in the village of Estarobon
2. The Trial — The village school of Estarobon
3. The Surrender — A city factory workshop
4. The Gunnery Lesson — A city factory yard
5. The Shot — A city factory yard

Part Two

6. The Trap — The Ruiz' house in the village of Estarobon
7. The Vendors — A road in the mountains
8. A discussion — A guerilla post in the mountains
9. The Arrest — The Ruiz' house in the village of Estarobon
10. The Soldier's Training — A clearing in the mountains
11. Human Cannon — Town Hall
12. The Smile — A road in the mountains

An interval after Part One.

Author's Note

This play has not yet been performed. During rehearsals for its first production I would probably make small changes to it but its discursive structure would be retained.

E.B.

Characters who appear in the first part of the play

PRIEST
AGUSTINA
TINA
NANDO
IGNACIO
PACO
CATALINA
TOMASO
MARCO
MIGUEL
GLORIA VERGARA
MARGARITA ARRANCE
VILLAGER 1
VILLAGER 2
VILLAGER 3
VILLAGER 4
VILLAGER 5
JUDGE 1 (IRENE)
JUDGE 2
JUDGE 3 (MIGUEL)
SENTRY 1 (TOMASO)
SENTRY 2
SENTRY 3 (MARCO)
GRANDMOTHER
ANTONIA
RICO
BLIND MAN
CRIPPLED MAN
WOMAN WITH SMALL GIRL
JUAN
GENERAL
BISHOP
CHAPLAIN
FACTORY MANAGER
ASSISTANT

Characters who appear for the first time in the second half of the play

JOSE ALBANA
MARIA
MANI
CORPORAL
PORTLY MAN
WIFE
SON (AURELIO)
HARRISON-LEIGH
FAWCETT
VENDOR
SOLDIER 1
SOLDIER 2
SOLDIER 3
PRISONER 1
PRISONER 2
ROSITA
GUADALUPE
PIO
INVESTIGATOR
CLERK
CIVIL GUARD 1
CIVIL GUARD 2
CIVIL GUARD 3
CIVIL GUARD 4
BERTA TORBADO
RENATA ORTIZ
NINA MIRAN
TERESA MARTIN
MARIA BARRIOS
RENATA RAMONES
MARIA CORVES
JUNITA MURCIANO

PART ONE

One: The Nameless Child

A house with a field sloping behind it.
    AGUSTINA *is in the house with her dead child.* NANDO *works in the field with their young daughter* TINA.
    The PRIEST *comes to the door. He is about thirty.*

PRIEST: Good morning. My housekeeper told me your child had died. I'm sorry.

AGUSTINA *pours water from a bucket into a bowl.*

She'll make you up a box of vegetables. Your husband can collect it at the funeral.

AGUSTINA: Send it. He's busy. (*She undresses the child and washes it.*)

PRIEST: Will he be long? You know Im often asked to send men up to do odd jobs on the estate. I cant recommend your husband over the heads of my flock. Tell him to come to church. What he does there's between him and his maker. It wouldnt be a compromise: he'd be paid for an honest day's work. You're too isolated up here. You see everything in black and white. If you werent so poor the child would have had a better chance of living.

The PRIEST *goes to the door.*

(*Calls.*) Nando!

TINA: The priest called.

NANDO (*making a wooden box*): Once there were two men. One day one of them went to the forest. There was a stone on the ground. Suddenly he saw that he could use it to cut down a tree. The stone was the first tool. Till then people had only collected fallen branches. Now he cut down four trees. Naturally his neighbour said 'I'll have one'. When the man said they were his, his neighbour said no they came from *their* wood and he took one. The man sat and pondered and his eye fell on the stone. Next time his neighbour came for a tree he killed him with the stone. The first tool became the first weapon. Give me the nails. (TINA *gives him the nail box and he counts out eight nails.*) Eight. (TINA *takes back the nail box.*) Next the dead man's family said we'll kill him. So the man cut down ten trees and brought home a pile of sharp stones and said to some of his other neighbours, take these stones and protect me. In return I'll give you some of my wood. They were the first policemen. Next the man used them to guard the trees he *hadnt* cut down. Now if you wanted wood you had to work for him. Soon the world became complicated but the story didnt change. At different times its a tragedy or farce or mystery but the plot is always the same.

The Argument of the Story (Nando)
When someone else owns the machines you use to earn your living then you are owned
Those who own the machines own the state, which is the system of ownership – and so they own everything
The result is terrible: When everything is owned everything becomes a weapon
Its as if even the tools you hold in your hand as you work turn into weapons you use against yourself

How can such a world be at peace?
People are angry and cruel not by nature – but because society requires anger and cruelty from its citizens
This is the argument of the story: when the machines are owned by those who dont use them everything becomes a weapon and the world's filled with enmity

NANDO *gives the box to* TINA.

TINA: Is it a true story?

NANDO: Yes – but all governments ban it. Your mother cant have any more children. Line it with hay.

NANDO *and* TINA *go down to the house.*

PRIEST: I'm sorry the child's dead. What was its name?

NANDO (*gestures* TINA *to give the box to* AGUSTINA): Everyone takes an interest in it when its dead. It hasnt got a name.

PRIEST: We'll need one for the Register.

NANDO: Its not being buried in the churchyard.

PRIEST: You mean to bury it in your field?

NANDO: I cant, I'd ruin my pick – you get to the rock after two inches. Anyway I cant spare the land.

PRIEST: Its your duty to protect your wife, not add to her sufferings. We cant know what a mother suffers when she loses a baby. Now when her body heals her mind will suffer even more if the child's buried in common ground. What's the sense in that? I'll send the doctor to her.

NANDO: We need a harrow if you could send that.

PRIEST: Your conduct is an offence to the parish! The behaviour of animals! You cant even bury your dead properly yet you complain you're not allowed to run your own lives! God save us from the day! I'll be in the vicarage till midday tomorrow. I'll tell the sexton to dig the grave. There wont be a fee.

The PRIEST *goes out right.*

AGUSTINA: I've taken the clothes to sell at the weekend.

NANDO (*as* AGUSTINA *puts the child in the box*): I'll be away overnight. If I bury it here they'd dig it up. I know a gulley where we camped when we were boys. Dropped stones in it.

AGUSTINA (*to* TINA): Put something to eat in your father's tin. (*Flatly as* NANDO *nails the lid on the box and* TINA *puts food in the tin.*) The pain doesnt stop after you give birth, it turns into the grief when you bury it.

NANDO (*kisses* AGUSTINA *and* TINA): Goodbye.

TINA: Shall I come?

AGUSTINA: No stay with me.

NANDO *takes his jacket, puts the tin in his pocket and the box under his arm and goes up the slope.*

Clear up for me.

TINA: Wont it have a name?

AGUSTINA (*half-hearing the question*): No it wasnt born in a human world, it was born in this world.

* * *

IGNACIO:
On the fifteenth of February nineteen thirty-six the Spanish Popular Front defeated reaction at the poles
The reactionaries began to plot
Franco had the appetite of the wolf
The caution of the snail
The eye of the hawk
And the arrogance of a man
After four months he revolted in Morocco with an army of thirty-six thousand
He had to move his army to Spain before the Popular Front could create an army to fight him
The Republican fleet blockaded Morocco
Franco sent messengers to Hitler and Mussolini
Within days fascist planes were carrying his army to Spain
The people's militia – poorly armed and untrained – stopped Franco forty miles from Madrid
The snail spoke to the wolf and Franco opened a new front in the north

In the first days of the fascist rebellion the villagers of Estarobon stood ready to defend the Republic
The landowner fled

* * *

Two: The Trial

A school room and a hut in Estarobon. Desks, chairs and benches in the school room.

A group of visitors, among them AGUSTINA, NANDO, TINA, IGNACIO, PACO, CATALINA, TOMASO, MARCO, MIGUEL, GLORIA VERGARA, MARGARITA ARRANCE.

IGNACIO: We need places for the judges, witnesses, accused, prosecutor, defender –

VILLAGER 1: These little chairs will give under our weight.

VILLAGER 2: They make them as tough as bar stools so the children cant break them.

The furniture is rearranged for a court. When it is done the adults sit in the children's chairs.

VILLAGER 3: Who has the teacher's desk?

TINA: The prosecutor!

NANDO: Judges!

IGNACIO: A revolutionary court doesnt use oaths. The enemy says that's because we're a rabble. No, in our court no one needs to lie! The facts arent in dispute, we have to decide the meaning of the facts! A revolutionary court's the only one that can give justice, the rest just tuck the rich up in bed. All our witnesses do is tell us how they live! Let them have the teacher's place!

VILLAGER 2: We're all judges.

AGUSTINA: We all have the right to speak but we need judges to run our court.

IGNACIO: A bag of stones picked up from our streets. Black or white. The first three to pick white are judges.

The VILLAGERS pick stones. Those who pick white stones hold them up in the air. All those who pick stones put them in their pockets. Quietly three judges are chosen.

These are the three.

JUDGE 1 (*a woman*): We didnt ask for the job but if you want us we'll do it.

VILLAGER 1 (*points at JUDGE 1*): Irene is stubborn.

JUDGE 2: She stands up for the right.

VILLAGER 4 (*points to JUDGE 3*): Miguel loses his temper.

JUDGE 1: Only when there's an injustice.

VILLAGERS: They'll do.

The judges take their place. IGNACIO *beckons* PACO *and* CATALINA *forward.*

JUDGE 1: Catalina, Paco: answer the questions and dont be afraid.

CATALINA: Why am I here?

JUDGE 1: This is a trial.

CATALINA: I havent done anything wrong.

JUDGE 3: You're a witness.

CATALINA: What will they do to the church? They're piling the pews in the street and throwing the statues and hymn books on top.

JUDGE 1: Let's begin.

SENTRY 1 *fetches the* PRIEST *from the hut.*

IGNACIO: Neighbours no court can be more just than the society in which it sits. Are there rich and poor, owners and workers? Then in that society there will be two of everything: schools, hospitals, houses and law – one for the rich and one for the poor. So if you want to know the court, look at the society. Today let's have a wise decision – and then we'll begin to respect ourselves after the years when we lived like their animals. (*To the* PRIEST:) These are your judges. D'you object to them? (*No response.*) I prosecute. Name someone to defend you.

PRIEST: Pablo, Luise, Im ashamed that you older members of the parish allow this to happen! The Marquis and the civil guard have run away – so you pick on me because Im the only one left.

JUDGE 1: You mustnt interrupt.

JUDGE 3: Please name someone. We want to be fair.

IGNACIO: You're charged with murder.

PRIEST: Ridiculous! Who have I murdered?

IGNACIO: Manuel Barrios.

PRIEST: Its disgraceful to use the poor man's death in this way.

IGNACIO: Paco, go to the teacher's desk. (PACO *cant be seen behind the desk.*) Stand on the chair. (PACO *stands on the chair.*) Tell us about the time in the orchard.

PACO: I was going to my aunty's. I have dinner at her house. Mr Barrios was in the orchard.

IGNACIO: What did he do?

PACO: His stream was dry. He was walking up and down it as if he was looking for something.

CATALINA: There never was such a time.

IGNACIO: Did he speak?

PACO: No.

IGNACIO: What happened later?

PACO: After dinner I came home. It was very hot. At first I thought the saddle was hanging on the tree. Mr Barrios was in his black suit and straight and the white ground hurt my eyes. Then I saw the rope round his neck. He was hanging from a branch and the saddle was on his shoulders. He'd put his cap on the ground. I ran to the bottom of the orchard and called him but he didnt answer. I went home. The civil guard put him in a cell in the police station. I dont use the orchard now when I go to my aunty's.

JUDGE 1 (*to the* PRIEST): D'you want to ask the boy anything? (*No response.*) Paco you can go.

PACO: Good.

PACO *runs out right.*

IGNACIO: Catalina go to the teacher's desk.

CATALINA: I dont know what you want.

SENTRY 3 (*takes* CATALINA *to the teacher's desk*): Sit down.

CATALINA (*cries briefly*): Its about Manuel. What can I tell you? (*She sits.*) Our land was hard to work. We were tired even when we got up. But we made a living. Then when we were old it was all taken away from us. As if a wind came one night and blew everything away. In the morning we were beggars. You youngsters do what you have to do. Im too old to understand. (*She gets up and walks away from the teacher's desk.*) Its too complicated to explain – yet its so simple I can see I cant do anything about it. Take me home.

IGNACIO: We're here to give you justice.

CATALINA: Too late.

JUDGE 1: D'you want others to suffer like Manuel?

CATALINA: No no god forbid.

IGNACIO: Then help us. You had a stream.

CATALINA (*nods, staying where she is*): It ran through the orchard. We dug gullies down to our field and blocked them off with stones. In the evening we lifted the stones and the water flowed down to us. It was a great joy. Better than ten sons. Sons work but –

IGNACIO: Tell us about the mortgage.

CATALINA: – they eat. With a stream you only have to pray for rain. When the work was too much for us Don Roberto gave us a loan. The steward came every week for the interest. Then every day. Manuel gave up making excuses. The steward said 'It'll have to be the water'. That Saturday they built the wall that stopped the stream running through the orchard. Concrete. The steward said we could fetch water but we're too old to fetch it. Now Don Roberto's tomatoes are full of our water. Our seedlings shrivelled up. Lay on the ground like dead insects. There never was such a time. (*She cries briefly.*) Why am I here?

IGNACIO: What did Manuel do?

CATALINA: He shrivelled up like our crop. His body frightened me. He was like a little monkey. Then he shaved and put on his good suit and hanged himself. There wasnt enough weight on him to do it quickly so he put the ass's saddle on his neck. What does god say to such things, father?

IGNACIO: You can go now Catalina.

CATALINA: And what good did it do Don Roberto? (*She laughs.*) He's run off like our water! Everything's upside down. Soon they'll have a square sun. (*She goes to a chair and dozes.*)

PRIEST: Agustina speak for me. They'll listen to you.

AGUSTINA: Me? Ask a churchgoer. Get someone who understands you.

PRIEST: They want to kill me. You know I didnt harm Manuel. I loved him.

JUDGE 2: If he wants your help you should give it Agustina.

AGUSTINA: Well – I'll do what I can. (*To the Judges.*) For a start he didnt take Manuel's water so why does he have to defend himself?

IGNACIO: A crime was committed. He was paid to look after the village's morals. What did he do about it?

PRIEST: What could I do?

AGUSTINA: You knew Serosan wanted the stream?

PRIEST: The whole parish knew. He wanted to farm on the hill so he needed water. He could have let his steward burn Manuel's house or set-up an accident to break his ass's legs – I've seen such things since I came here – but Manuel was old and it would have caused comment. So he gave him a mortgage, knowing he couldnt pay it back. That way he got the water legally and the village didnt complain.

AGUSTINA: What did you do?

PRIEST: When my housekeeper told me the steward was worrying Manuel every day I went to the Marquis as his spiritual adviser and told him he was endangering his soul. It could have been a nasty interview. I spoke without hope.

AGUSTINA: Didnt he listen?

PRIEST: He always listened to a priest. But he said the economy was depressed. Capital wasnt investing because they didnt like the liberal government. Strikes in the cities. Terrorism. The law had to be enforced. He had other mortgages and the people who owed them would take any leniency he showed Manuel as an excuse for not paying. As I told you, I spoke without hope. The Marquis acts on what he was taught are the principles of a christian gentleman. The law must be enforced with rigour because it must be feared: the church is the fountain of mercy – and so he endows it with money. He said the mortgage had given Manuel a year on his farm and now the church should put him in one of the almshouses he paid for.

AGUSTINA: What did you do?

PRIEST: You will laugh. I prayed for the village.

AGUSTINA: Did you go to anyone else?

PRIEST: There was no one else.

AGUSTINA (*to the* VILLAGERS): Yet the whole village knew what was happening. (*To the* JUDGES:) Why didnt you do something? Suppose the village had decided to stop Serosan stealing the water. You could have burned his crops. Poisoned the stream. The government wouldnt have sent troops. If you have to go to that extreme to uphold the law you do more harm than if you neglect it. They'd have stopped Serosan stealing the water. Or you could have clubbed together and paid Manuel's debts.

VILLAGERS: No no!

AGUSTINA: No because some of you would have said what about my mortgage?

VILLAGER 1: We're worse off than Manuel! We've got children to feed.

VILLAGER 4: We need new tools. A new roof.

AGUSTINA: And then you'd have sat hunched over your fists which are worn down like spent flints yet still empty – and finally realised how much you had to do! But you did nothing. A priest's power depends on persuasion but your power is your strength when you act. Suppose he'd spoken from the pulpit? The bishop would have shut him up. He couldnt have done anything, he takes on obedience with the cassock. But you could have spoken on the streets in the clothes you're wearing now – and you can make far more noise on the street than you can in the pulpit! But you did nothing. You're worse than the priest, you're as bad as the Marquis.

JUDGE 1: Well Ignacio, what's your answer to that?

IGNACIO: Manuel was illiterate and so he couldnt leave a suicide note. I'll try to speak for him. The theft of this water was as blatant as if one of you had coshed him on the street and taken his wallet. You'd have been charged with murder. Yet the Marquis was allowed to profit from his crime! Agustina if we'd burned the crops Manuel would still be alive but we'd be in prison. Our land would be neglected and Serosan could buy it up dirt cheap. Who gives him his money? The papers – in which he owns shares – say he works for it. As hard as two men? Three? Ten? No one could work that hard without dying of exhaustion – and anyone who says he could has never done a day's work! Yet Serosan has the money of a thousand men! You get that by theft. There is no other way. Men like him steal all they have. How? The law keeps them rich and us poor. We work to make them rich enough to employ us! When we obey their law we commit a crime: we allow their thieving to go on, and with it all the waste and ignorance that make this world sordid – and hanged Manuel. To maintain so much injustice almost every truth has to be corrupted. Those who do it get paid, but worse – they do it in good faith. Priests, officers, teachers, men who call themselves philosophers and scientists, editors, judges, public oracles – they look at this terrible world and say men are beasts and without us their state would be even worse. And we – we are the people who allow this to happen! Why? Because we have founded our lives, our acts, our characters on believing their falsehoods. We have become their cattle. Forgive me, I have waited years for this day. (*Slight pause.*) Then neighbours, is our situation hopeless? The dyer's hands are stained by his dye. If one day there is no more dye the water is clear. But his hands are still foul. How will he make himself clean? By washing his hands in the water that dyed them! How else? We change ourselves by struggling to change our society. That's how we become human. There is no other way. I accuse the priest – not because he said we'd get justice in another world but because he makes the injustice of this world possible! He doesnt fire the gun. He's the silencer on the gun.

VILLAGER 2: My mother couldnt get treatment! Serosan went to a sanatorium to get rid of his fat!

VILLAGER 3: We protested when he raised our rent! After that our son couldnt get work!

NANDO: They keep a blacklist!

VILLAGER 4: My husband joined a strike in the city. They put him in prison. It took a civil war to get him out!

JUDGE 2: Wait – wait –

JUDGE 3: If you all tell your story we'll never finish.

VILLAGER 4: We've heard enough.

VILLAGER 3: Shoot him!

JUDGE 1: Agustina.

AGUSTINA: There are a lot worse priests. He sees both sides. He's at home with rich and poor. But what sort of man can go from a house where a family is crowded together, eats badly, has no privacy and no time to think but has to live as if the world ended at their doorstep – to a house where everyone eats well, has their own room and enough clothes for ten families, and there are gardens to rest in, and time to read and think and learn how to fool or force the people in the poor house to provide all this for you? He might be wandering from one continent to another, one century to another, but all this takes place in one parish. He even wanders between worlds! When he's bewildered he runs to god like a child running to mother with a grazed knee. He's learned nothing from the twentieth century, yet tells us how we should live in it! He believes bread turns into meat, the dead come to life, virgins can fly. He also believes little children are born guilty of the sins they havent yet had time to commit. That if long ago an old man hadnt murdered his son we'd all spend eternity burning in hell – and some of us will. What sort of man is he? He's mad. No sane man could believe such things. Well the insane arent responsible for their crimes. Let him go. Good riddance. Soon he wont have any power over us.

VILLAGER 2: There wouldnt be this talk if we were Serosan's prisoners!

VILLAGER 4: That's how they get their power!

VILLAGER 2: They always use violence when they cant get what they want without it!

VILLAGER 3: What's the verdict?

VILLAGER 1: Sentence!

VILLAGER 5: Stand him against the wall!

The villagers are silent.

JUDGE 2: We cant shuffle our feet.

JUDGE 3: He's as guilty as hell.

JUDGE 1:
We sat in court and searched for justice
It was as if we polished a silver plate that had lain in the soil for years
Where it had been buried when our village had been pillaged and put to the sword
Now we see ourselves in the silver
And we say he is guilty and sentence him to be shot

JUDGE 3:
But we do not ask the people to knock down the wall that makes Manuel's small field as dry as a dead lizard
The water still sparkles in the light as it hurries over the stones
And it has covered the barren hillside with maize and red and green peppers and brazen corn
Let the river stay and the new fields go to the villagers

JUDGE 2:
The tree on which Manuel hanged still bears fruit
Let us pick it and give it away in the market
His tomb shall not be a place of shame
But a monument to this just decision

PRIEST (*to* AGUSTINA): Ask them to let me pray.

JUDGE 1: He can pray.

The three sentries put the PRIEST *in the hut and fasten the door. They stand guard.* CATALINA *sleeps.* PACO *runs in from the right.*

PACO: They're burning the church. They took the paraffin from the stores and threw it up the walls. They let me throw a candle on the fire!

JUDGE 2: Dont set fire to yourself!

PACO *runs out right and the other villagers follow him.* GLORIA VERGARA *comes on from the left.*

GLORIA VERGARA (*with pan*): Look. Copper. Weighs a ton. Half the village are at Serosan's house.

SENTRY 1: We said no looting.

SENTRY 2: The Marquis looted it from us.

SENTRY 3: There should be a proper share-out.

PRIEST (*in the hut*): My sons dont murder your priest. The secret fraternities will take revenge. Follow you night and day. They swear an oath that –

SENTRY 2 (*kicks the hut*): Pray!

GLORIA VERGARA: They're stripping it bare. Walls. Floors. Ceilings. Piling everything on the carts from the stables.

SENTRY 2 *goes out left.*

SENTRY 1: What about the farm machinery?

SENTRY 3: Those who suffered most should get first pick.

MARGARITA ARRANCE *comes in from the left.*

MARGARITA ARRANCE (*with cushions*): Look. Embroidered gentry hunting in a forest. I'll get home from work and put that under my bum.

GLORIA VERGARA: Copper.

MARGARITA ARRANCE: We'll all have pans now. I'll never get another chance to have something like this. Girls went blind making those stitches.

SENTRY 3: Our women'll be up there. They'll get our share.

SENTRY 1: He had farm tools from America. Tools like that save labour – you live longer! We sit here two hours and that's costing us our life!

SENTRIES 1 *and* 3 *go out left.*

PRIEST (*in the hut*): Boys, unfasten the door. I must stop them burning the church!

GLORIA VERGARA (*to* MARGARITA ARRANCE, *finger to lip*): Sh. (*She wakes* CATALINA.) Talk to father. (*She points to the hut.*)

GLORIA VERGARA *and* MARGARITA ARRANCE *go out right.*

PRIEST (*in the hut*): Who's there?

CATALINA: They're all gone, father. What are you doing in the hut?

PRIEST (*in the hut*): Catalina god's sent you to save the village. They'll all suffer if they harm me. Open the door.

CATALINA: They seemed sorry for Manuel. I didnt mean to harm you father. If they –

PRIEST (*in the hut*): God has forgiven you. Now thank him by opening the door.

CATALINA: They ought to take me home.

PRIEST (*in the hut*): How is the door locked?

CATALINA: A spike's wedged against the hasp.

12 HUMAN CANNON

PRIEST (*in the hut*): Catalina you're old. You'll need a priest when you die. Take the spike out.

CATALINA: Gloria Vergara's stolen one of Don Roberto's saucepans. She'll cop it when he gets back.

PRIEST (*in the hut, crying*): O god, Catalina please. Please.

CATALINA: In the morning you go round the traps. The creatures inside stare at you through the bars. You take them out and knock them on the head or lower the cage in the stream. (*She tries the spike.*) Wedged.

PRIEST (*in the hut*): Use your strength woman! (*He rattles the door.*) Quickly! Quickly!

CATALINA: I cant open it if you kick the door. (*The door stops shaking. She struggles with the spike.*) The barber's radio says the roads arent safe. You run away. I dont want to make them angry for nothing.

CATALINA *opens the door and the* PRIEST *comes out.*

PRIEST: God will bless you. Say your prayers.

The PRIEST *starts to go, comes back, shuts the door, puts the spike in the staple and goes out.* CATALINA *wanders back to her chair.*

CATALINA: I shant hang. I said to Manuel 'You're too proud. What's the use of that? Beg!' I dont care what they think of me. (*She dozes off.*)

SENTRIES 1 *and* 2 *come on from the left.*

SENTRY 1 (*with a gaming table, bangs the lid*): A gaming table full of dice. His chauffeur had a set of stainless steel wrenches. I bet kids are playing with them!

SENTRY 2 (*with cutlery*): Silver cutlery with saints' heads. We'll flog this junk in Barcelona. Get a good price in the docks.

VILLAGERS *come on right.*

SENTRY 2: Comrades he's had time to pray.

IGNACIO: Do we go through with it?

NANDO (*to* SENTRIES 1 *and* 2): Someone else can take your place.

SENTRY 1: We'll do it.

SENTRY 2 (*goes into the hut and comes out*): He's gone.

Others look in the hut.

AGUSTINA: Who opened the door? When?

SENTRY 2: I went to the big house to stop the –

SENTRY 1: Shut up!

NANDO: You left him alone?

SENTRY 2: No the other two were there. Otherwise I wouldnt have –

SENTRY 1: We went to rescue the farm machinery. The village needs –

NANDO: Where's Marco?

IGNACIO: Looting!

SENTRY 1: No, guarding the house! We went to –

IGNACIO: Saboteurs!

VILLAGERS: Saboteurs!

NANDO: Take their guns!

SENTRY 1: No!

IGNACIO: They cant be trusted with guns!

VILLAGERS *disarm* SENTRIES 1 *and* 2.

SENTRY 1: Comrades we shouldnt have left our – but we're not traitors!

SENTRY 2 (*to* SENTRY 1): Why did you leave him on his own?

SENTRY 1: There was a crowd about. We thought it was safe. The door was bolted.

SENTRY 2: Who opened it? The wind didnt do it!

CATALINA: I did. I was sorry for him. I told you to take me home. You know I lost my wits when Manuel hanged. (*Holds out her hand like a beggar.*) Help an old woman.

IGNACIO: Put them on trial!

NANDO: What's the use of trials if prisoners get away?

NANDO, IGNACIO and VILLAGERS: In the hut!

SENTRY 1: Comrades!

VILLAGERS: In the hut!

SENTRIES 1 *and* 2 *are put in the hut. The door is shut.*

SENTRY 1 (*in the hut, banging on its door and sides*): The good life's beginning.

SENTRY 2 (*in the hut, banging on its door and sides*): Let us share it!

Pause. It is quiet in the hut; the men inside are listening. Outside the MEN *silently load their rifles.*

SENTRY 2 (*in the hut*): We'll catch the priest, comrades . . .

SENTRY 1 (*in the hut*): . . . He cant be far . .

Silently the VILLAGERS *aim at the hut.*

NANDO: Fire! (*Volley. Shouts from in the hut.*) Learn how to live! (*Volley. Shouts from in the hut.*) Learn how to live! (*Volley.*) Learn how to live!

VILLAGER 3: Fire lower!

IGNACIO: No they'll cling to the roof.

Two stray shots.

NANDO: Wait. (*He strikes the side of the hut. Silence. He kicks open the door and goes in. He comes out carrying* SENTRY 2.) Take him to the Murciano's house. She's saved people before.

VILLAGERS 2 *and* 4 *start to carry* SENTRY 2 *out. (Cf. Goya's wounded workman.)*

VILLAGER 2: Gently.

VILLAGER 4 (*to* TINA): Hold this in the wound.

VILLAGER 4 *gives* TINA *a cloth and she walks beside* SENTRY 2 *plugging his wound as* VILLAGERS 2 *and* 4 *carry him out right.*

NANDO: Tomaso's dead. Shoot me if you want.

IGNACIO (*looking off left*): Marco. Shall I shoot him with the grin on his face?

MARCO (SENTRY 3) *comes in left. He is grinning.*

MARCO: Comrades, have you been in the big house? Enormous! Our hospital – or factory! There's a swimming pool with huge glass walls to close in the winter! (*Shows guitar.*) Look mother-of-pearl in the handle and a silk strap. I never thought I'd play a guitar. I shall take lessons! (*He plays chords.*)

NANDO: Look in the hut.

MARCO (*looks in the hut*): Was there an attack?

NANDO: You left your post.

MARCO: There were people about – we thought it was all right to –

NANDO: It's useless to say that! You just went!

MARCO: I see: the good times have come! The comrades shoot each other. (*Lifts rifle.*) Not me!

NANDO: Put it down.

MARCO: You shot my mate!

NANDO: The anger's gone, it was used up. Bury him. (MARCO *goes into the hut.*) The Marquis left in his fast car. Then a private plane. He banked abroad, he'll live well. And the priest slid behind him like his shadow. There are priest holes everywhere. We'll try to find him. We're pushing down a prison wall with our bare shoulders. When it falls we have to straighten up quickly or we'll fall with it. This is the first day of the war. I hope its the worst.

MARCO *has come from the hut carrying* SENTRY 1. *No one helps him. He goes out right, with the other* VILLAGERS *clustered round him.* CATALINA *is last. She holds out her hand to beg from the dead man as he is carried past her.*

* * *

TINA:
For three years the people's militia slowly retreated before Hitler Mussolini and Franco
In December nineteen thirty-eight Barcelona fell
Soon Madrid would fall
And on the first of April nineteen thirty-nine the Republic would fall.

* * *

Three: The Surrender

Factory compound.
Large, bare, light. Noises of machines and

goods being moved in metal trolleys.
  A GRANDMOTHER *sleeps in a deckchair. Beside her is a bag with a few personal things.*
  ANTONIA *comes in left.*

ANTONIA: Mother come to the canteen.

GRANDMOTHER: Not hungry.

  AGUSTINA *and* TINA *come in right.*

ANTONIA: You dont know when you'll get your next meal.

GRANDMOTHER: 'S too noisy.

  ANTONIA *goes out left.*

AGUSTINA: Your father asked me to wait for him here. He says its the only quiet place in the factory: the glass roof would be dangerous in an air raid so its not used. We've been walking through the city this morning. We havent walked together for so long. Even before the war. You marry and settle down. A child comes. You meet at meals and talk about the day's problems.

TINA: You two have always been like one pair of eyes.

AGUSTINA (*laughs*): Have we? This morning we stood and held hands on the bridge. I let my hair down. I'd forgotten how it suits me. There were gulls squabbling and starlings strutting up the quay. I havent seen the world like that since I was a girl. Everyone looks happy. The enemy's coming but they're not here yet. No one works to make someone else rich. No one's confused by the lies they used to call the news. People even dress more casually. No ties, only a few buttons. Before they went about the streets as if they were visiting the sick. Now they walk as if they owned the earth – no, the sky. Freedom makes you happy. We said it would. Not many people will have it. But everyone who was in this city will always think of those who werent as strangers.

  ANTONIA *comes in left with a tray on which there are three bowls and three spoons and three slices of bread.*

GRANDMOTHER (*to* AGUSTINA): Where're you from my dear?

AGUSTINA: Estarobon. You wont know it, it's only a little village. This is my daughter. We're both visiting our husbands. We havent seen them for a year!

ANTONIA: Rice with peas in it. Rico's coming to eat with us.

GRANDMOTHER: Antonia married my grandson.

ANTONIA (*to* AGUSTINA): There's food in the canteen if you hurry. (*She puts a bowl and spoon in* GRANDMOTHER's *hands.*) Take your spoon.

TINA: D'you work here?

ANTONIA: I started in D shed when I left school. Now I'm in H. I met my husband in the explosives block.

GRANDMOTHER: I'm seventy-one. When I was born only birds and insects flew. And a few saints they say. Now men fly about dropping bombs on us. I cant find any peas. The rain makes the glass roof green. Where the stain runs out of the metal, see? This is like a conservatory. When I was a maid the doctor and his wife had breakfast in the conservatory.

ANTONIA: At night you can see the moon through the glass. Its like looking into a river. When we were both on night shifts I used to come here for five minutes with my husband.

TINA: Why is the factory so crowded?

GRANDMOTHER: They're people from the working class area. If we dont surrender their houses'll be shelled.

ANTONIA: They cant get out of the city. The roads are blocked by convoys. Franco wont bomb the factory – its as safe as a bank. Private property. Besides he needs the shells.

AGUSTINA: I've never seen such a busy place. The machines are working and they're stacking shells in the loading bays. But one shed's been turned into a nursery: children playing in circles, babies at the breast, toddlers with rattles. There's a laundry in the basement. They hang the sheets and nappies between the sheds and wheel the shells out underneath them. Some of the corridors have been curtained into sections to give the families somewhere private. Upstairs there's a ward full of patients. Some of them have been wheeled onto the roof for fresh air. There's even a dentist with a barber's chair. And a library. And part of the stores has been turned into a school. The children have taken the chalk they use to mark up batches of shells and they're writing alphabets on the walls. The factory's like a town.

RICO *comes in. He wears military uniform.*

ANTONIA: Is the meeting over?

RICO: As good as.

ANTONIA (*takes away the slice of bread covering his bowl*): Eat this before its cold.

RICO (*eats*): God Im hungry. We'll surrender. No fighting. Our troops move out tonight. The fascists move in in the morning.

GRANDMOTHER (*to* RICO): You see if you can find my peas.

TINA (*to* RICO): What will you do?

ANTONIA (RICO's *mouth is full*): He'll go with the army.

RICO: In a year or two the whole of Europe will be at war. We can hold out until then. When the allies fight the nazis they'll have to fight our fascists.

TINA (*to* ANTONIA): What about you?

ANTONIA: I'll go on working here. They always need trained labour.

GRANDMOTHER (*hands bowl to* RICO, *he empties it into his bowl*): They're good children. They wont leave me.

NANDO *comes in. He wears military uniform.*

RICO (*to* NANDO): I told you it was all over.

AGUSTINA: D'you want to eat?

NANDO: They'll surrender the city. It would cost too many lives to defend. Play for time till the big war. Good. But they wont blow up the factory. It makes shells! No wonder we're not winning! They say they cant get the people out. Turn them out with bayonets! If the city surrenders they'll be safe in their homes. They dont *want* to blow it up! They'd lose their jobs! (*He gestures to* RICO.) He'll let his wife go on working here! One of her shells could kill him!

ANTONIA: I've worked in armaments for eight years. I know all the arguments. We need work: we have to live. That's my argument.

RICO: She has to earn so that she can eat and take care of my grandmother. What else can we do? If my number's on it I'll cop it – which'd make some other poor bastard happy. Look, if she didnt make the shell someone else would. So if Im going to be killed at least let her get the benefit of the money. I hope its not a dud so I go quick.

NANDO: If we lose the war that doesnt mean –

RICO: I'm going to see if there's any more grub.

RICO *goes out left.*

GRANDMOTHER: Why is the man angry? Does he want to turn us into the street?

ANTONIA: Its all right, Granny. Everything's decided. They'll let the workers stay here. When the Fascists come they'll surround the factory and let us out through a checkpoint. No one will be on their list – if they were they'll have left with the army. The well-off will stand on the pavements and jeer but we'll walk home between them and pretend not to notice.

GRANDMOTHER: I'm going to sit with the old people. They cant turn us all out. (*She starts to go left.*)

RICO *comes in left. The factory begins to go quiet as the machines are switched off.*

RICO: There're crowds camping on the streets. The gates are shut. No more are allowed in. The sanitary orderlies say it wouldnt be hygienic – and the food would run out. Go and look! Its like an army. The factory's under siege. Even if they cant get in they feel safe if they can touch the walls.

NANDO: If we lose the war that doesnt mean we've lost everything. Not if fighting the war made us stronger – freer – more determined. Then even if we lost this one we wouldnt be defeated! But if you help them now we've got nothing from fighting! We've had our chances and we're worse off than before! We had no right to ask our comrades to die!

RICO: How could you move that crowd from outside!

NANDO: This is not just betraying our revolution, its betraying all revolutions! We're chucking freedom back in people's faces!

RICO holds out his hand to NANDO. *The* GRANDMOTHER *comes back.*

RICO: Comrade, there's been enough quarrelling.

GRANDMOTHER (*to* RICO): Why're you shaking hands? You're going to let him turn us out! They'll shoot us on the streets!

ANTONIA: No one will turn you out – I told you. Go and sit with your friends. We'll come and see you.

GRANDMOTHER goes out left. RICO still holds out his hand.

NANDO (*turns away*): There's comrades' blood on it.

RICO (*to* ANTONIA): The troops must leave soon or we wont get out. Let's find somewhere quiet to say goodbye.

From the right a BLIND MAN *pushes in a* CRIPPLED MAN *in a three-wheel bath chair. The* CRIPPLED MAN *guides the wheel chair with a rudder attached to the front wheel. On his lap there is a violin in a case and a flute.*

CRIPPLED MAN: We came in through the little door we used in the old days. The directors' cook was good to us. (*To the* BLIND MAN.) Stop. She gave us her scraps in the evening.

BLIND MAN: We wont be a nuisance.

RICO: You cant stay. The sanitary orderlies –

CRIPPLED MAN: You wont notice two more. I'm the Crippled Man who leads and he's the Blind Man who pushes. We're famous. The poets praise us!

RICO: There's a danger of an epidemic.

BLIND MAN: But we had our picture in an American newspaper!

From the right a WOMAN *comes in carrying a full shopping bag and leading a* SMALL GIRL.

WOMAN WITH SMALL GIRL: Im looking after the little girl. Someone tried to snatch my bag and frightened her!

CRIPPLED MAN (*to the* BLIND MAN): Idiot you said you'd bolted it!

RICO (*going right*): I'll bolt it.

RICO goes out right.

WOMAN WITH SMALL GIRL: The little girl isnt mine. She lost her people in the war.

CRIPPLED MAN: All this space!

ANTONIA: You cant use it – the roof makes it dangerous!

BLIND MAN: I'll jam the brakes.

CRIPPLED MAN: If I dont lead he cant push! (*To the* WOMAN WITH THE SMALL GIRL:) Mix in with the others. They cant catch you!

BLIND MAN: We'll earn our food and keep your spirits up!

CRIPPLED MAN: Straight ahead!

The WOMAN *and the* SMALL GIRL *go off left. The* BLIND MAN *pushes the* CRIPPLED MAN *off after them. The* CRIPPLED MAN *plays a snatch of a popular tune.*

NANDO: They've switched off the power. The families will sit by their machines till their enemies come and switch them on and then go back to work. They might as well be making their own chains.

TINA: Slaves have to make their own chains. If they saw the owner doing it they'd know what he was and get rid of him. You shouldnt have got angry. If the shells dont kill him they'll kill his friends even if they're fired at his enemies! The owners get workers to fight for them, kill each other for them, orphan each other's children. In the end all weapons are used against the working class. And it wouldnt make any difference if this factory was making sewing machines. They'd be working for their enemies. That means – you said – that all tools turn into weapons they use against themselves. The slave makes his chains. In our society everything is a weapon – so you have only one way of making a living: beating ploughshares into swords. That's why we need a revolution. Then the weapons could become tools again, and we could build instead of destroy. Isn't that what you taught me? I'll come to you in the morning.

NANDO: Walk with us some of the way. I havent seen you for so long.

TINA: My husband's waiting for me. Goodbye.

TINA *kisses them and goes out left.*

AGUSTINA: Can you stay the night?

NANDO: Yes. I'll go early in the morning before its light.

AGUSTINA: I shant go straight back to the village. I'll try to get work here. I can organise the factory girls. We must eat. If I cant find something to cook in this city I couldnt bump into a dark wall at night with my eyes shut.

NANDO: I'll take you back to my place. Its over a cinema. Guess what? It's got a dome. And a wide window ledge – you sit out there with all the statues on the roofs round you and look down at the streets.

* * *

AGUSTINA:
The poor dont ask the shopkeeper to give his food away
The prisoners dont ask the governor to set them free
Students dont ask to be taught understanding in an hour
No one tries to pick the fruit while the blossom's on the tree

Howling in the desert will not bring one drop of rain
And weeping over dead men will not make them live again
Yet you cry aloud for peace as you hand the knife to Cain
And peace to the war dogs who are pulling at the chain

Nation will fight nation till there is justice between nations
And that will not be till there is justice within nations!

Till then the workers will make guns and quietly eat their bread
And will not see the marks of Cain and Able on their head
The warlords will praise peace by the wargraves of their dead
And madmen will be rulers in the land of the insane
And the world will call for peace and the call will be in vain

* * *

Four: The Gunnery Lesson

Factory Compound.
75 mm gun and a sentry in Fascist fatigue uniform
AGUSTINA *comes in from left.*

AGUSTINA: You'll be glad when the war's over, soldier.

JUAN (*bored*): Hop it.

AGUSTINA: I work here. This is my lunch break. Before you liberated us we couldn't stroll in the sun after lunch. Had to work for the officers. Wash shirts, clean boots. When you moved in it was like watching Lazarus come back to life.

JUAN (*bored*): Funny no one you speak to was on the reds' side.

AGUSTINA: That uniform suits you.

JUAN (*bored*): D'you want to be run in?

AGUSTINA: Its the truth. You take care of yourself. Dont waste it on the first skirt that comes along.

JUAN: Chance would be a fine thing.

AGUSTINA: There's more rooms in a house than a bedroom. You want a woman who can cook and look after you.

JUAN: Scram you old cow.

AGUSTINA: Im not doing any harm. You're from the south.

JUAN: How d'you know where I'm from?

AGUSTINA: All the real Spaniards come from the south. Its a long time since I talked to a man who wasnt complaining about the mud on his boots. Your people are farmers.

JUAN: Wrong – not our own land. The estate hires us. For the harvest. Then no work till next year.

AGUSTINA: Will you leave the army after the war?

JUAN: Men and flies. No machinery. Took

six weeks. I'll stay in the city when Im demobbed.

AGUSTINA: There'll be a lot looking for work.

JUAN: I'll be all right. I've got a training.

AGUSTINA: What as?

JUAN: Motor mechanic. Surprise you?

AGUSTINA: No I knew you were clever.

JUAN: Guess where I learned?

AGUSTINA: Some university. Madrid.

JUAN: Self taught.

AGUSTINA: Motor mechanic? You cant be!

JUAN: Watched the proper mechanics. Looked in an engine every time I got a chance. Fix my officer's when it breaks down. Its all right for him: he doesnt pay. I dont mind: its the best way to learn. He says I was born with a spanner in my hand.

AGUSTINA: I bet your mother's proud of you.

JUAN (*shrugs*): My brothers'll never get off the land, I'll be able to send her good money from the city. She's had a hard life. When she's washing up her hands are all crinkles. I used to think you're too old to be my mother.

AGUSTINA: You can pay her a visit when you've settled down.

JUAN: We'll see. It's a long way.

AGUSTINA: I know you lads like a bit of fun – you've earned it – but if you ever feel like a quiet evening with a good meal, you're welcome at my place. My husband was killed in an air raid. We had no children. The house gets a bit lonely. I mustnt bother you.

JUAN: The war hurt a lot of people. Thanks for the invitation. We're not allowed out on our own.

AGUSTINA: Bring a mate.

JUAN: We'll see. Well you'd better move on.

AGUSTINA: Yes, thanks for talking to me.

JUAN: That's all right.

AGUSTINA: One day you'll have your own garage.

JUAN: I don't know about that – costs money.

AGUSTINA: Im not often wrong. Anything's possible with a lad like you.

JUAN: I might take up flying.

AGUSTINA: There you are – you're clever! That's why you knew which side to fight on.

JUAN: To tell you the truth they just lined us up on the square and marched us off to be kitted out. You have to hand it to them, they've got it organised. When the reds get an order they vote on it. Our officer said when you reach their lines they'll have one hand up voting on whether you're coming. Soldiers shouldnt have opinions, they're just a liability in war. If our officers changed the enemy they wouldnt bother to tell us thank god – I've got enough to think about. Today its the reds, tomorrow it could be the greens. Its got nothing to do with me who we're fighting. Kill or be killed, that's all it is. Discipline not bloody opinions.

AGUSTINA: I can see you've got it all worked out. What would you do if there was an attack?

JUAN: Now? Blow the whistle and cock this. (*Rifle.*)

AGUSTINA: Wouldnt you fire that? (*Cannon.*)

JUAN: No shells. Only issued in an emergency.

AGUSTINA (*looks at the cannon*): Yes you'd have to be specially trained to fire that. Not easy like a rifle.

JUAN: I can fire it.

AGUSTINA: Dont be ashamed, you cant know everything.

JUAN: Im not ashamed!

AGUSTINA: I couldnt fire it and I'm not ashamed.

JUAN: Well you're a woman. Look you'd better get back to your girlfriends. You'll get a reputation talking to soldiers.

AGUSTINA: I can stay a bit longer, Im not due back yet. (*She looks at the cannon.*)

All those knobs. I'd forget which end the shell went in.

The Gunnery Lesson

JUAN: You know the difference between your back door and the front door dont you? Well the shell goes in the front door – and you close it after you. (*He opens and shuts the breech screw.*) That's what the LBM's for: loading breech mechanism. Shut LBM – then turn till grooves on screw lock with grooves on ring.

AGUSTINA: The front door! You'd make a good teacher. If you stayed on after the war they'll make you an officer.

JUAN: Its just a question of finding the right language.

AGUSTINA: What's that?

JUAN: Elevation gear. To aim with. You dont aim at the target, you aim beyond it.

AGUSTINA: Beyond it?

JUAN: Because of the parabola.

AGUSTINA: What's a parabola?

JUAN: Well you have to know a bit of theory. Suppose you hang your washing on the line. You dont start in the middle and work outwards do you. The rope'd sag. Then your sheets drag on the ground and you have to wash them again. So you start at the ends and work to the middle. That's taking a parabola into account. Only with shells its the other way up.

AGUSTINA: Imagine I've been doing that all these years and didn't know!

JUAN: Now you see that? That's the sights. Mostly you cant see the target. So you aim at something you can see – you call that your gun aiming point – and someone who can see your gun aiming point and the target tells you the difference between the two. You feed the difference into the sight (*Demonstrating.*) but turning it the opposite way from the target. The barrel doesnt move. Then what d'you do?

AGUSTINA: . . . Turn the sight back to the aiming point but this time move that barrel-thing with it.

JUAN: Brilliant! And then the barrel's laid – that means aimed – on the target.

AGUSTINA: Suppose I want to hit those gates. I'd aim at the window.

JUAN: No they're close. You can aim straight at them.

AGUSTINA: That would be easier.

JUAN: You'd use the telescope. You know about your elevation gear. But you could still go wide. So you use your traversing gear. Suppose you want to hit the tower on the Police HQ. (*He points at the telescope.*) Look through that. Go on, it wont hurt you. (AGUSTINA *looks through the telescope.*) See the laying mark in the centre of the glass? Ignore all that grid for the time being. Now align it so that the laying mark is on the base of the tower – then you'll pull it down on top of itself and not just blow the lid off. Use your gears. Go on. (AGUSTINA *operates the gears. He takes her place at the telescope.*) Bit more left. (AGUSTINA *looks through the telescope.*) Turn the traverse gear (AGUSTINA *turns the traverse gear.*) – there you go. (*He takes her place at the telescope.*) You're on target.

AGUSTINA: This morning all I could do was thread a needle. Now I can fire a gun!

JUAN: Wrong. Load and aim it. Not fire it.

AGUSTINA: I knew it'd be too hard for me.

JUAN (*indicating*): That's the firing lock. You put the firing tube in the breech screw. Inside the lock there's a striker. When you pull the firing lever the striker strikes the tube – the tube fires gunpowder at the shell – and you're off. As easy as striking a match. See the angel on the church?

AGUSTINA: You mustnt, its sacrilege.

JUAN: Its not loaded. (*He looks through the telescope and turns the gears.*) Target laid. Open breech screw. Insert shell. Close LBM. Turn LBM. Insert firing tube. Close lock. Release firing lever. Bang. Angel sees it coming and flaps off.

AGUSTINA (*laughs*): I bet you're a laugh in barracks.

JUAN: You try.

AGUSTINA: Shall I?

JUAN: It wont bite you. (*He spins the elevating and traversing gears at random.*)

You're on your own now. If I keep telling you what to do you'll never learn. Just say to yourself its no harder than remembering what order you put in the ingredients when you're cooking. Now we'll see if that meal's worth coming round for.

AGUSTINA (*operating the cannon*): Target laid. Open that thing. Put the shell in. Close it. Bugger's stiff. Put in the firing tube. Close lock. Release lever. Bang.

JUAN: No.

AGUSTINA: What did I do wrong?

JUAN: You didnt turn the LBM.

AGUSTINA: I told you I was stupid. (*Operating the cannon.*) Open screw. Shell in. Close LBM. Remember to turn it. Put in the firing tube. Close lock. Release lever. (*Quiet contentment.*) It clicked . . . I heard it click . . . it fired. Open screw. Shell in. Close LBM. A good turn. Insert firing tube. Close lock. Release firing lever. Click . . . it fired again. Open screw. Shell in. Close LBM. Remember to –

JUAN: We wont do it anymore. You can damage the lock without a round. You could go on to study ballistics, artillery strategy – there's a lifetime of study in it.

AGUSTINA: You could teach anyone anything.

JUAN: You dont have to fawn on people. Its not nice for a grown woman. Respect yourself like a real Spaniard. Your husband was from the south wasnt he?

AGUSTINA: Yes.

JUAN: If I can get out one evening I'll come round for a meal. I need a change from canteen food. My corporal might even come.

AGUSTINA: I'll write my address and give it to you next time I see you. If you need any socks darning just give them to me. I enjoyed my lunch break today. (*Going.*) If your officer caught you chatting at me you'd be for it.

JUAN: *You* were chatting at *me*. According to Regulations I'm entitled to run you in just for saying good morning. (*Calls after her.*) And what about the recoil? You didnt stand off when you fired. You'd be broken in half by now.

AGUSTINA *goes off left.*

* * *

ANTONIA:
From time to time Agustina spoke to the lonely soldier. Not every day, to arouse his suspicion. Sometimes she only nodded. At others she gave him his darned socks neatly folded round a bar of chocolate. She didnt speak again about the cannon. Many distinguished visitors came to the factory to gaze at the workers or demand more shells. Agustina said: they shall not sleep in their beds, they shall hurry through the streets like criminals fleeing from their crime, their possessions shall not give them the joy of use but the fear of loss. And she waited.

* * *

Five: The Shot

Factory Compound.
75mm gun and sentry in Fascist parade uniform.
AGUSTINA *comes on with a bucket of water with a yard broom in it and a bucket of polishers and rags with a yard broom laid across the top.* TINA *follows her.*

JUAN: Agustina hop it. You cant come here today.

AGUSTINA: Its all right the foreman sent me. (*To* TINA:) The top brass is unveiling a plaque inside. The factory's role of honour in the struggle for fascism. (*To* JUAN:) The bishop loves soap next to Jesus. I washed this floor till its clean enough for him to celebrate mass on. Now I've got to do it again.

JUAN: Who's the girl?

AGUSTINA: My lodger.

JUAN: Well get on with it and no chatter.

AGUSTINA *and* TINA *go to one side and clean.*

AGUSTINA (*quietly to* TINA): Antonia will go by when they're leaving.

TINA: Sh, dont speak.

AGUSTINA: He expects women to chatter. If we dont he'll get suspicious.

(*To* JUAN:) You polish your buttons as well as I clean this floor and they'll make you a general. (*Quietly to* TINA:) Leave him to me till I rattle the pail. Then you start. (*To* TINA *loudly:*) That's Juan.

JUAN (*to* TINA): Hello lovely.

AGUSTINA (*to* TINA, *loudly*): Watch him he's got hot blood.

TINA *goes on working.*

JUAN (*to* TINA): Where've you been all my life? (*No answer.*)

AGUSTINA: She's not shy when she talks to me. You should have heard her just now. (*To* TINA:) You're as bad as the girls on the bench. All they talk about is soldiers. (*To* JUAN:) I thought I was normal but they make me blush.

JUAN: Agustina dont go on. You're embarrassing.

AGUSTINA: Lovely isnt he? I have a job to keep my hands off him.

JUAN: Agustina. (*Aside to* AGUSTINA:) I can do my own chatting-up.

AGUSTINA (*to* TINA): That's what I call a real Spaniard. And he knows it.

JUAN: Not in front of her.

AGUSTINA (*gestures at him with her broom*): Shoosh! She's only blushing because she fancies you. Dont you Camilla?

JUAN: She hasnt said so.

AGUSTINA: You havent said you fancy her but you do. Look at him drooling over your breasts. In the evenings she strips and stands on the towel and washes herself in my kitchen. You should see the water running off her breasts. I stop and have a look. I had a pair like that when I was her age. All the men trying to touch them. (*She smacks his rear.*) The army's bulging on the centre front.

JUAN: D'you sleep with Agustina?

AGUSTINA: O she's got her own room. Everything private.

JUAN: Why dont I come round for that meal Agustina? My corporal's a pal. He'll let me out if I slip him something.

AGUSTINA: There you are! I've been inviting him for weeks. Always tomorrow. Now he's drooling, and not for my paella. Will your corporal let you out all night?

ANTONIA *walks from left to right.*

JUAN (*to* AGUSTINA): Get a move on and less lip. (*He points.*) Look at that dirt.

AGUSTINA: Where?

JUAN: There. I want that spotless.

ANTONIA *goes out.*

What about Wednesday?

AGUSTINA: Too late. You've just liberated her village and she's off to nurse her grandfather. Good thing too. Now she's seen you she'd soon be in trouble. You wont get anything off her. So enjoy looking.

JUAN: Does she have to go?

AGUSTINA: He wont sleep for thinking about your tits. You should see the water running off them. Since the young men have been away the poor girls dont stand a chance: breathe down their necks and they're yours. You'd have added her to your list Juan. They're all different inside, they say. You'll never find out what she's like. She might have been the best. (*She laughs.*) It doesnt bear thinking about. (*She sweeps.*) At my age you take it or leave it. But look at you two: standing there shivering and looking at each other like two herds of cattle. (*She goes to one side, rattling her pail.*)

JUAN: Where's your village?

TINA: Near Vigo.

JUAN: Christ. Cant you put it off for a few days?

TINA: I've got a lift on a lorry. Everyone wants to get home. I darent let the chance go . . . Agustina's always talking about you. That's why I came.

JUAN: If it wasnt so open.

TINA: I know.

JUAN: Put it off one day.

TINA: Its the lorry.

JUAN: I'll get you a lift on an army truck.

TINA: I couldnt risk it. The lorry driver's from our village, he'll look after me.

JUAN: Christ woman dont stand like that.

TINA: Couldnt you – (*She stops.*)

JUAN: Yes! What?

TINA (*points*): Behind there.

JUAN: Im on sentry duty.

TINA: Agustina will keep watch.

JUAN: All right. But wait till they go.

AGUSTINA: Dont be long Camilla. If they catch you here there'll be hell to pay.

TINA: The girls say some of the sentries . . . in the sentry box.

JUAN: I've done that lots of times. Its – there's a general inside.

TINA: You could say you went to look at something suspicious.

JUAN: I have to blow my whistle first.

TINA (*turning to go*): Pity.

JUAN: Wait.

TINA: I shouldnt have come. I cant go home like this.

JUAN: Look – if we're quick, behind the wall. I'd be fantastic with you. (*He changes his mind.*) No – its mad. I'll tell you what: I've got some leave money due. I'll pay your train fare. Take a week's leave and we'll spend it in bed.

TINA: Its poor grandfather you see.

JUAN: Oo you little darling. All right then – the wall. Look – I'll stand on the corner – you go behind the wall – and do me with your hand.

TINA: There's no satisfaction in that for me Juan.

JUAN: Goddam you bitch! Sod you. But be quick.

AGUSTINA *gestures to indicate that she will keep watch: looks over her shoulder at them and jerks her right fist forward with the thumb raised.* JUAN *and* TINA *go behind the wall.* AGUSTINA *waits.* JUAN *comes back.*

Christ this is lunacy! I've gone mad!

TINA *comes round the corner with her blouse undone.*

Jesus woman there's a bishop inside! Do your blouse up! He'll crucify me! (*Pause. He goes to her.*) Sod you. Sod you. You cow.

TINA *and* JUAN *go behind the wall.* AGUSTINA *picks up her buckets and brooms and goes to the cannon. As she talks she aims the cannon, takes a shell from under the rags in the bucket and loads it.*

AGUSTINA: A woman with a bucket and mop is invisible. Today I ply the ancient trades of whoring and cleaning. The soldier follows his ancient callings of fornication and war. Inside his general unveils a plaque to the fallen. A paper-thin tombstone on a wall. My daughter will be shy. The soldier will be anxious. She'll say Agustina's keeping watch. And soon he'll forget time. In their passion men are like victims running in burning clothes from a fire: they cant see where they're going for the flames they bring with them.

From the left come the GENERAL, BISHOP, *his* CHAPLAIN, *the* FACTORY MANAGER *and his* ASSISTANT. AGUSTINA *cleans the cannon.*

GENERAL: They didnt cheer.

CHAPLAIN: My Lord Bishop has a sobering presence.

GENERAL: Cheering's good for morale.

ASSISTANT: We told them not to take time off to cheer.

MANAGER: We're on target to double production by the end of the first period.

BISHOP: Our workers are still bewildered. We must be patient and strive for their understanding. Words count for little. When they are fed and clothed and cherished they will cheer us.

CHAPLAIN: Thank you for those words of wisdom father.

GENERAL: You can cheer and work.

They go out right. AGUSTINA *is alone. She adjusts the aim on the gun.*

AGUSTINA: What will the soldier do? Run back pulling up his trousers, turn and run up and down between the sheds cursing and roaring like a wounded animal, like a fish threshing on top of the basket trying to find the hook to show why he was tempted. Soldiers will surround him as he stands there shouting and pointing with his trousers round his ankles. He'll be court-martialed and shot. His owners take their time: the managers bow, the general salutes, the chaplain rubs his hands and the bishop gives his blessing. In a moment some of them will be killed or lose a leg or an arm. Or they may all be killed. By a shell that didnt leave the factory in which it was made.

AGUSTINA *fires the gun: there are two detonations, the firing of the gun and the explosion of the shell.* AGUSTINA *goes out left.* JUAN *runs on. His trousers are round his ankles and he is trying to pull them up. He waves his rifle and blows his whistle. He stops for a moment and stands in the smoke and roars like a wounded animal. Then he turns and runs off.*

End of part one.

PART TWO

Six: The Trap

The house.
A trap door in the floor is open with the stone cover beside it.

AGUSTINA:
The Marquis and I have returned to Estarobon
The people took back the loot: not to the house
Instead they left it along the road
Strange sight! As if the countryside were the Marquis' house
In a field a circle of *quinze* chairs: empty when the sun rose and when it set
Tapestries and curtains hung on rocks: no hand or breeze parted them
Pots and pans on a tree: as unused as in a painted kitchen
A woman returning from work drank from her cupped hands not the crystal glass by the stream
Children sang but the lid of the portable organ with the marquetry cherubs was as shut as a lid in the grave
The owner drove back to his house and sent out his gangs
They returned with his loot: he checked each item against his lists
He charged the community for what was missing.

NANDO *comes out of the trap.*

NANDO: I can hide here for a few weeks – I'd be safe for years.

As NANDO *and* AGUSTINA *talk he goes in and out of the trap taking down pillows, blankets, food, utensils.*
AGUSTINA *keeps watch at the window.*

AGUSTINA: They've searched some houses ten times. They wont find you. The stone's too thick to sound hollow. I can only buy food for one: the police have told the shopkeepers to report anything suspicious. Dont worry, I'll feed us. And no reading: the smell of a candle would give us away.

NANDO: What'll you do when I go?

AGUSTINA: Carry on as before. The cellar can be used again. You'll need to organise an escape route to the mountains. If any –. The priest on the path.

NANDO *goes down the trap and replaces the cover, using the iron handle on the underside.* AGUSTINA *fetches a broom, sweeps dust round the edge of the cover and treads it in. She puts the broom away and works in the kitchen. The* PRIEST *comes in.*

PRIEST: Good day. (AGUSTINA *nods.*) Have you heard from your husband?

AGUSTINA: No.

PRIEST: I expect he managed to cross the frontier. Is your daughter coming to live with you?

AGUSTINA: She's better off at her in-laws. They can feed the child when it comes. This place is so run-down it hardly feeds me.

PRIEST: You know the army's investigating everyone in the parish. You were one of the group considered today. Your husband and your son-in-law were rebel officers and your views are well known. I had an excuse to speak on your behalf because you defended me at my trial. However there was little I could say. This house and the land were confiscated. You're free to live anywhere else in Spain. Go to your daughter.

AGUSTINA: They cant support me.

PRIEST: Let me finish. They've dealt with you less harshly than they have with many others. No doubt there'll be complaints. Its better for your own sake if you go.

AGUSTINA: Where to? God knows I'm out of their way up here.

PRIEST: That was the decision.

AGUSTINA: I cant go.

PRIEST: Agustina you accept nothing unless its what you want. In a month you'd have the village seething. Organise meetings –

AGUSTINA: I've finished with all that.

PRIEST: Even if that were true you'd be blamed for everything that went wrong. Its better for the community that you go.

AGUSTINA: That's christian charity!

PRIEST: I saved your life. The truth is there's already been a complaint from the mother of the man who was shot in the hut.

PART TWO   25

AGUSTINA: I didn't shoot him!

PRIEST: When blood is spilt it calls for reckoning in its own kind. I cant protect you. You have to leave now.

AGUSTINA: Now?

PRIEST: Your house has been given to Jose Albana. He's bringing his things up in a cart.

AGUSTINA: I cant leave now.

PRIEST: Realise how fortunate you've been. I asked to be allowed to tell you so that you could leave quietly. There could be a squad of soldiers here!

AGUSTINA: Its tyranny – to turn me out like this! I need time to arrange things. Just a few days.

PRIEST: What is there to arrange? Everything was confiscated.

AGUSTINA: My personal things. Photographs, letters –

PRIEST: Private Albana will put your personal things in a box and the army will mind it till you send for it.

AGUSTINA: I wont go! I have to let my –. Cant I walk round my own field once! Of course I'll go. Thank you for speaking for me. Let me stay one night. One night. On my own.

PRIEST: Nowadays everything's done quickly. Perhaps that's god's kindness: it may be better if we dont have time to think what's happening to us.

JOSE ALBANA *and his wife* MARIA *wheel on a small handcart holding a few possessions: utensils, a holy picture, bedding, clothes and so on.* MARIA *starts to unload.*

JOSE: Agustina. We're really appreciative. You're not leaving the place to vandals. Maria will keep it as spotless as if you were liable to pop in at any moment to inspect us. It ran down during the war . . . With a young couple to get it going . . . I had a look round the other day when you were at the village. We'll have our work cut out.

MARIA (*hands* JOSE *a box of cutlery*): Put that in the table drawer.

PRIEST (*taking a case from the bottom of the wardrobe*): Agustina's clothes can go in this.

MARIA *takes clothes from the wardrobe and drawer and packs the suitcase.* JOSE *goes on unloading the cart and bringing things into the house.*

AGUSTINA: Maria let me have the house for one night. I came here when I was married. My daughter was born here. Five minutes notice. Its cruel. Come back in the morning. I'll cook breakfast for the three of us. Then you'll come in as friends. Not like this.

MARIA: Agustina let's get it over for everyone's sake. We all have to start from the beginning again.

AGUSTINA: You can wait one night.

JOSE (*coming in with his gun*): No its an order.

MARIA *shuts the case and gives it to the* PRIEST.

PRIEST: O Jesus who dwelt in the abode of the simple carpenter, bless this house and all who dwell here. O Jesus who had nowhere to lay his head, take the homeless into thy care. Amen. (*To* AGUSTINA:) You can take your coat.

AGUSTINA *takes her coat and holds it in her hand as she goes out with the* PRIEST. *He carries her case,* JOSE *and* MARIA *finish unloading their things and wheel the cart to the side of the house.*

MARIA: If she does something silly it'll bring us bad luck. What if she –

JOSE: Dont start! Im not quarrelling on our first night! For god's sake if you dont like it go somewhere else! (*Pause as they work. Consolingly:*) We'll talk about it tomorrow. She wont do anything silly. That one's tough.

MARIA: Be careful with the blankets.

JOSE: Its our house now. We were ordered to take it. There arent many hands as clean as ours. You've got a good kitchen. You always said the other one was too small. I hope now there'll be some decent grub. I'm sorry I shouted.

MARIA: Its so cut off.

JOSE: Who wants to live under their neighbours' noses?

MARIA: If only it was nearer the village. I wouldnt –

JOSE: Things'll be quiet now the army's in charge. I dont want to hear another word.

MARIA *prepares a small shrine: portable reredos and idol. She lights a candle at the shrine and kneels before it.* JOSE *sits on the edge of the bed and takes off his boots.*

They had all the speeches. They'd do this, they'd do that. The big shareout. Boots would polish themselves. Now what? He's dead and she's on the street. I should have written their speeches: 'Brothers things have got to change. But not in our lifetime. Admit it and enjoy what there is. A bed, roof, food in the cupboard, a winter coat. Who wants the freedom to be shot?'

When the shrine is complete he perfunctorily crosses himself in front of it.

AGUSTINA:

**The Curse
(Song)**

You set each man against his brother
You hire the father to fight the sons
You drive the daughters from the mother
The workers live by making your guns
You teach the child to walk in darkness
Your city is the gate of hell
You price men by their heap of money
Or by the blood they have to sell
   The earth groaned when you sat on your thrones
   And it will still groan when you are dead
   Because it must find you a place for your bones
   May the stone lie heavy on your head!

JOSE *and* MARIA *are in bed in the darkened house – only the candle is lit.* NANDO *comes from the trap and goes towards the door.* JOSE *gets out of bed and reaches for his gun.* NANDO *sees him and takes the gun.*

NANDO: Dont move.

JOSE: Is there a tunnel?

NANDO (*half to himself*): Why didnt he sleep?

JOSE: Nando. I wont say you were here. Your friends would kill me.

NANDO (*as before*): Why? Why? I couldnt wait any longer.

JOSE: Nando. You went to school with my father. You're like my uncle. Talk to me.

NANDO (*as before*): Why didn't he sleep?

JOSE: I tried to. It was the excitement. I was planning our future. I owe the house to you Nando. Now I'll owe everything.

NANDO (*as before*): Why, why is it always the same? (*To* JOSE:) Is Maria asleep?

JOSE: Yes – she wont be any trouble. She does what I tell her.

NANDO: I'll take you behind the rocks. The noise will wake her but she wont see me. She wont have to suffer.

JOSE: Nando for god's sake!

NANDO: Quiet! I cant trust you, you're a civil guard.

JOSE: I needed the job.

NANDO: I went through everything while I waited. Backwards and forwards for hours. Give me one reason to trust you.

JOSE: I'm a worker like you. I wont say a word, I'll be so grateful. Nando you said when I was little: 'an honest boy'. Uncle Nando please. O why didnt I pretend to sleep?

NANDO: Give me one reason.

JOSE: Let's think quietly. Now – take me on the path. Tie me up. Gag me. I'll say I heard a prowler. Went out. Didnt see who it was.

NANDO: That's not the point! I need a reason to trust you! Hurry. I must be in the hills before its light.

JOSE: O yes! Shoot me! Like the men in the hut!

NANDO: Jose, I dont want to kill you! Give me a reason! Help me!

JOSE: Of course, of course! What a fool! Why didnt I see it? No one knows you were here – so you *werent* here! There is no problem!

NANDO: There is! I cant trust you!

   JOSE *throws a chair at* NANDO *and runs for the door.* NANDO *shoots him. He falls.* MARIA *sits up in bed.*

MARIA: Jose!

NANDO: Turn to the wall.

MARIA (*gets out of bed; she is naked*): What is it? (*She goes to* JOSE.) O! He's not – he's breathing!

NANDO: Dont look at me.

MARIA: Help me Nando!

NANDO (*lowers gun*): He's dead.

MARIA (*cries quietly*): O god.

NANDO: Maria I'll trust you, you dont need to betray me.

MARIA (*after crying quietly for a moment*): I'll betray you! You shot him! Animal!

NANDO (*quietly*): Look at this gun that killed your husband. Now listen. He said he wouldnt say I'd been here. But tomorrow? To please his CO? Promotion? A bigger house? He worked for the Fascists, how could he be trusted? They dont even know Im alive. If he talked they could have followed me to my friends. Shot my wife for hiding me. It was her or him. You understand?

MARIA: What?

NANDO: Listen. A man came in from the yard. He didnt speak. Scarf on his face. Shot Jose and left. Give me your word.

MARIA: I promise. (*She takes the idol from the shrine and holds it to herself for protection.*) I promise Nando.

NANDO: Good. Get into bed. (*She gets into bed, still carrying the idol.*) Cover your head with the blanket. Pretend to sleep. Wait till its light. You were too afraid to go for help before.

NANDO *replaces the stone cover, fetches the broom, sweeps dust round the opening and treads in it.*

MARIA (*under the blanket*): What are you doing?

NANDO: Pretend to sleep.

MARIA (*under the blanket*): I told him not to come to this house.

NANDO *puts the broom back in its place. He hesitates.*

MARIA (*under the blanket*): I wont tell them it was you.

NANDO *goes to* MARIA *and shoots her through the head under the blanket. He leaves the house and goes out left.*

*   *   *

NANDO:
The priest put my wife on a train
A soldier waited on the platform till the train left
She looked out of the window at the darkness
There were no lights in the countryside
She might have been looking into the eyes of a skull
Rain slanted over the window
The skull was weeping

At Zaragoza she sat on the platform
And waited to be told I was dead
In the afternoon soldiers came and she was arrested
The station master had telephoned the barracks
She said she knew nothing
After six months they let her go.

*   *   *

Seven: The Vendors

Mountain Road.
   From the left, marching in loose order, come CAPTAIN MANI, *a squad of* SOLIDERS *and two* PRISONERS. MANI *wears a pistol, the* SOLDIERS *carry rifles and the two* PRISONERS *carry a machine-gun, its tripod and an ammunition case.*
   MANI *is short, thin and dark with a thin black moustache. He wears a képi with a small crucifix in place of the crown stud.*

MANI: The mountains of Spain. The sun rises out of the mist like the host being lifted up in a glass hand.

CORPORAL: Men fall out for a smoke Captain?

MANI (*shout*): Smoke!

CORPORAL: Fall out!

   The SOLDIERS *fall out and smoke. The* PRISONERS *stand by the machine-gun. A* SOLIDER *smokes and guards them.*

MANI: Die here! – in all this space you cant think of death: not in a wet cellar or on a municipal wall where everything tells you you're dying.

   From the right comes a PORTLY MAN, *his* WIFE *and* SON *and two English businessmen.*

PORTLY MAN: Captain is this the right road?

MANI: Its over. We're on our way down to the truck.

PORTLY MAN: Over?

SON: I said it was shooting.

PORTLY MAN (*to* HARRISON-LEIGH *and* FAWCETT): Its over! What a nuisance! We got up so early!

FAWCETT: The walk did us good. What a view! Worth getting up for that. Really.

WIFE: And I hurried you out with no breakfast.

FAWCETT: We werent in the least bit hungry.

MANI: Come tomorrow.

PORTLY MAN: Our English visitors go home tomorrow. (*He sits and fans himself with his hat.*) Now the war's over we're working to regain the confidence of our foreign friends. Low wages, people weary of politics and queueing up for work: we have all these advantages to offer. But they wont invest in us if they think there'll be another round of confiscations. I wanted to show them how the new Spain is ridding itself of its enemies once and for all.

HARRISON-LEIGH: Have no fears, we've seen enough to have every confidence.

PORTLY MAN (*to* MANI): I should have arranged it with your colonel. These gentlemen are the proprietors of the Windsor Accumulator-Battery Company. We intend to manufacture their modern Accumulator-Battery under concessionary license. The Government likes wirelesses. They keep them in touch with the people. As the economy leaps ahead every home in Spain will have its set. (*He fans his face.*) Its hot so early.

From the left a VENDOR *wheels on his stall. It has a tarpaulin top and paraffin burners. He stops and busily rattles cutlery and glasses as he pretends to clean his counter.*

PORTLY MAN: I was hoping to sign a contract this afternoon. I thought that seeing this – they're not used to war – would give them a jolt. Might get better terms. D'you know my factory? Vacancies at all levels. If you have any relatives . . .

VENDOR: Beefburgers.

SOLDIER 1: Dont get settled, we're going back.

SOLDIER 2: At least he could let us finish a fag.

SOLDIER 1: Christ hasnt crucified enough poor buggers this morning.

MANI: I've got two more prisoners.

PORTLY MAN: No no I couldnt bother you like that.

MANI: They're condemned.

PORTLY MAN: No no not at all not at all.

WIFE (*to* HARRISON-LEIGH): I do hope the concession goes through. My husband tells me our son will study in your factory. It would be so good for his English.

VENDOR: Wine.

PORTLY MAN: Is it those two?

MANI: They should have been shot last week. I let them carry the ammunition. Its not good to keep them too long. They learn the routine and work out how to escape.

PORTLY MAN: If you're sure. It sounds almost like doing them a kindness.

MANI: On your feet!

Subdued murmurs of protest from the SOLDIERS.

SOLDIER 2: Sun's up, Captain. It'll be like an oven before long.

MANI: Corporal! We're taking the English visitors to see the bodies.

SOLDIER 2: They dont need a guide. Even the English couldnt miss them.

PRISONER 1: You dont need the gun, Captain.

MANI (*to* COPRORAL, *indicating the prisoners*): And them.

CORPORAL (*to the* PRISONERS): And you!

FAWCETT: Dont go to this trouble for us. (*Aside to* HARRISON-LEIGH:) O lor', old Ramiro's fixed something up with the little captain. Just a moment –

The PRISONERS *try to run away.* SOLDIERS *stop them.*

SOLDIER 2: All right Sonny!

PRISONER 2: No!

SOLDIER 3: Bastard!

MANI: Your comrades didnt run. The dogs stood and cursed us. (*He points left.*) That's your road! We only borrow our lives! The time comes to hand them back!

PRISONER 1: Captain I want to see a priest!

PRISONER 2: The priest!

MANI: Infidel lies! You think you know how to dangle me on a little string. If you havent prayed this week you dont know how to pray!

PRISONER 2 (*to* HARRISON-LEIGH *and* FAWCETT): Englishmen – sirs – its cruel to treat us like this!

PRISONER 1: We're not animals.

CORPORAL (*detailing* SOLDIERS): You: gun. You and you: ammo. (*He gives the tripod to another* SOLDIER.) Carry that.

FAWCETT (*to the* PORTLY MAN): Look we dont want to distress anyone. Thank the little captain but tell him we –

HARRISON-LEIGH: Bambury please.

MANI: Corporal get a grip on your men.

CORPORAL: At the double – run!

PRISONER 2 (*to* HARRISON-LEIGH *and* FAWCETT): Give that to my wife. Please. (*He throws an envelope on the ground.*)

HARRISON-LEIGH (*to* FAWCETT): Dont make things awkward for our host. This is just the sort of sensitive area the Foreign Office man spoke about. (*He picks up the envelope and hands it to* MANI.) We observe the same strict neutrality as our government.

SOLDIERS *double out with the* PRISONERS. MANI *follows them.*

VENDOR: Beefburgers. Wine.

PORTLY MAN (*to* HARRISON-LEIGH *and* FAWCETT): They're murderers. The officer explained to me they'd have been shot anyway when they got back to barracks. (*To his* SON:) Aurelio order some iron rations to fortify us on the way. (*To* HARRISON-LEIGH *and* FAWCETT:) Imagine that spectacle every morning, knowing its going to happen to you. Doesnt bear thinking about. And the ammunition weighs a ton. (*He calls to his* SON:) Wine too. (*to* HARRISON-LEIGH *and* FAWCETT:) This early just once: then you can tell your wives you misbehaved in Spain.

SON (*at the stall*): Mother, anything?

WIFE: Certainly Aurelio, our guests cant eat on their own.

SON (*to* VENDOR): Five.

WIFE (*to* HARRISON-LEIGH *and* FAWCETT): In the war we took refuge in our convent. The nuns told them no one was hiding there. The shutters werent opened for three years. The cellars were crowded with poor wretches. At any moment the mob might have broken in.

PORTLY MAN: Dont distress yourself darling.

WIFE: We must never forget it. It was the Buddhists' Nirvana. We ceased to exist, we were shadows. When my daughter went out after the incarceration she'd forgotten there were streets between houses. Can you imagine? It was on her doorstep but she might have come from another world. We should ask why such things are possible.

PORTLY MAN *and* WIFE *go to watch the food being prepared.*

FAWCETT: Will we give him the concession?

HARRISON-LEIGH: No. Its cheaper to make them in Lagos in spite of the cost of freight. And safer.

FAWCETT: Shouldnt we tell him?

HARRISON-LEIGH: No the rest of the day would be embarrassing for all of us. We'll put it off till we leave. Dont worry, Tubby has other irons in the fire. He'll make a fortune out of trinkets for tourists.

SON (*to the* VENDOR): Good meat. Not scraps. The Police watch standards now.

VENDOR: Its a pleasure to serve a discriminating young sir. I enjoy it more than eating myself. A double for the Englishmen, yes? Those rumours about food shortages. Let's show them!

PORTLY MAN: Two bottles of red.

SON: Wipe the glasses.

The VENDOR *uncorks two bottles of wine and puts the corks back loosely in the necks of the bottles.* AGUSTINA *comes on right. She uses a walking stick and has a pear-shaped knapsack on her back. The* VENDOR *glances at her.*

HARRISON-LEIGH (*to* FAWCETT): Spain is a land of Tauromaquia and guerilllas. Those two didnt expect anything better. Its the way they do things here.

VENDOR (*to* PORTLY MAN): There's brandy for the Englishmen when you come back. (*He points.*) Excellent Valadamos.

PORTLY MAN (*calls to* HARRISON-LEIGH *and* FAWCETT): They should be ready for us.

PORTLY MAN *leads the way out left with a tray holding glasses and two bottles. The* SON *follows with a tray of food.*

WIFE (*to* HARRISON- LEIGH *and* FAWCETT): Arthur, Bambury, each take an arm. The last few steps are steep.

HARRISON-LEIGH *and* FAWCETT *each take one of the* WIFE'*s arms and go out left.*

AGUSTINA: I come round the side of a mountain and there's a street vendor!

VENDOR (*without looking at her*): I know about gypsies who ask for dog scraps and eat it themselves. Shove off from my counter. The English are fussy. Came in my shop before the war, if they found a spot of dust you'd think they'd won Waterloo again.

AGUSTINA: Your grub smells good. I'll have one. (*Money.*)

VENDOR: O sorry. (*He prepares a beefburger.*) You meet the cream of the riffraff up here. Beggars. Children thinner than half a matchstick. Cut your throat to lick the knife. First your heart breaks, then you feel the bits sticking in you, then you dont feel anything any more. (*He uncorks a bottle.*) Wine?

AGUSTINA: If its on the house.

VENDOR (*corks bottle*): There's water in the stream. Take it from further up. Its contaminated down here. I call this pitch my branch shop. I was lucky to get it. They wanted their cut: not just the captain, the colonel. Its worth it, thank god: I've got to pay off the bank loan. The crowd come up here to put the lid on the war. They want to celebrate with a drink. Before the war I had a bakery. My cakes were famous: pistachios and chocolate. The nobs sent taxis from the other side of town for them. Then the reds took it over. Asked me to stay on as manager. Same wage as the oven boy. I said fine, now I can keep an eye on it. Then they closed me down. No pistachios, no chocolate, no flour. (*He gives her the beefburger.*) *Bon appetit.* I took the family south. My boys fought for Franco. One of their officers said work in our mess and you can bake your famous cake. One evening I was serving and he said your sons are dead. Land mine got both of them. I went on handing round the cake – what else? Their mother cried for a week. Women cry better than men. With them its music. So she cried for the two of us and I listened.

Off, a burst of machine-gun fire. It rattles on the rocks.

AGUSTINA: An execution. (*She puts down her beefburger.*)

VENDOR (*astonished*): Woman where have you been for three years?

AGUSTINA: You sell food here?

VENDOR: A baker doesnt ask who eats his bread. At least when they're eating they cant do much harm. Eat. You paid.

AGUSTINA: How many?

VENDOR: Today? Fourteen, not counting those two. At the start it was forty and fifty a time. Real hard cases. Marched. Clenched fist. They could have been parading for their dead comrades. (*He wipes the counter.*) God death can be dramatic. I was worried the crowd might get fed up. Ha! They became afficionados, bet on who'd shout slogans. Dressed up like a holiday crowd. The prisoners die in rags. Leave their good stuff to the others still in prison. Spain must have the best dressed prisoners in the world. Eat. It'll get cold. When the troops aimed the crowd shouted fire. You cant blame them, they'd lost family and friends. Once they shot seven women. When the troops aimed they threw their skirts over their heads. Some insult, cover their eyes – dont know why. Anyway I always remember it: that was the best day's business I've done. Soon they'll do it in the barracks and no one'll know. He'll garotte. He's mad. First shooting he did sent him potty. Off his head ever since. (*He pours wine for her.*) Drink. Eat. (*Off, two pistol shots.* AGUSTINA *doesnt eat or drink.*) You think its wrong to trade here. If I sold to the same people in town would that be different? Do investors – or workers – ask what the company makes? They ask about money. The town goes about its business and down the road or up the hill they're stockpiling bombs: one day they'll blow kids' heads off. The town doesnt come to a halt. All you see here is yourself.

HARRISON-LEIGH *and* FAWCETT *come on from the left.*

FAWCETT: We shouldnt have left so soon. Old Tubby'll gloat.

HARRISON-LEIGH: We did our duty. If we'd stayed any longer it might have looked as if we took an unhealthy interest in that sort of thing. Then they'd all gloat.

VENDOR: Good wine, sirs – no? (*They ignore him.*)

FAWCETT: Wait till I tell the old man. Stared straight in front of them like people waiting on a railway platform. I wouldn't have imagined that at all. Usually onions are – well, arms all over the place. Really Arthur it was just like when I had to put Roger down. Fell over and wriggled a bit and then sort of shrank. Only he wagged his tail, poor bugger. Wouldnt do to have missed it though. A very important thing.

PORTLY MAN, *his* WIFE *and* SON *come on from the left.*

VENDOR: Gentleman now for our choice Spanish brandy – to improve the view. (*No response.*)

MANI *comes on from left.*

PORTLY MAN: It would have been silly to waste the climb. The *jeunesse dorée* comes up here in their open Lamborghinis. More money than sense.

WIFE (*to* HARRISON-LEIGH *and* FAWCETT): This afternoon I shall take you shopping for gifts. Next time you must bring your ladies with you to Spain. I insist.

PORTLY MAN: Gentleman, brandy to drink to the Windsor-Toledo Accumulator Battery.

HARRISON-LEIGH (*slightly cocking his head to the right and gently raising his right hand to hold it a few inches from the side of his face with the tops of his fingers in line with his eyebrows and the palm facing forward*): Bit early I'm afraid.

SOLDIERS *come on from the left with the machine gun, tripod and ammunition case.*

MANI: Gentlemen. When the prisoners asked for a priest they slandered the regime. Its true that at the start we werent organised and once or twice a priest couldnt see the prisoners in time. But the prison was paraded and the priests absolved all the prisoners together. Perhaps dying in terror makes brutes like these repent when otherwise they wouldnt. We shorten their lives but give them eternity.

AGUSTINA (*eats*): Baker you can cook! This meal will last me a lifetime!

VENDOR *smiles and goes out left.*

HARRISON-LEIGH (*to* MANI. *Handshake*): Well turned-out body of men.

FAWCETT: Very interesting thing. Very important.

MANI (*clicks*): Thank you. I vowed that if I fell into my enemies' hands they'd throw their hats in the air when I told them my name. Soon I'll go into a monastery. A simple place where they grow vegetables in the cloisters and there's one bell. Then I can read and become a monk. I've done my duty for eight years, but that's what I've always wanted. O I dont want to forget: I carry all those we shot in my head all the time so that when I go to heaven and stand in the little crowd that's waiting to be welcomed, my maker – who sees all – will see the dead in my head and smile at me. Long live death!

SOLDIERS: Long live death!

MANI: Christ the king!

SOLDIERS: Christ the king!

> VENDOR *comes in from the left with the trays and empty bottles and glasses.*

VENDOR (*to the* PORTLY MAN *as he pockets the tip from the tray*): Many thanks.

MANI (*to* SOLDIER 1): Check her.

> MANI, SOLDIERS, PORTLY MAN, *his* WIFE *and* SON, HARRISON-LEIGH *and* FAWCETT *go out right. The* VENDOR *follows them, pushing his stall.*

SOLDIER 1: Where d'you think you're going?

AGUSTINA (*eats*): Valencia. I've come from Urgel.

SOLDIER 2 (*takes her knapsack and looks into it*): Why?

SOLDIER 1: Pass.

> SOLDIER 2 *takes* AGUSTINA*'s pass from the knapsack and hands it to* SOLDIER 1.

AGUSTINA (*eats*): To join my daughter. My husband disappeared in the war. Sat on a mine or ran off with a woman.

SOLDIER 1 (*giving the pass back to* AGUSTINA): Whats wrong with the trains? They run on time now.

SOLDIER 2 (*giving the knapsack back to* AGUSTINA): But she cant afford the ticket.

SOLDIER 1: Watch out for the guerillas on top.

AGUSTINA (*shrugs*): They wont bother me. Wouldnt be worth their while.

> SOLDIERS 1 *and* 2 *go out right.* AGUSTINA *goes out left.*

* * *

Chorus

You who smile and live well
Hear what the outcasts can tell
You keep watch from the ramparts on your walls
But you have locked your enemies inside your gates
No one is free in your city
Fires will ignite on the empty streets
Your cities will burn and you will fall
You who smile and live well
Remember what the outcasts can tell
The ring of your coins as you buy and sell
Tolls like the notes of a funeral knell
And your cities will turn into hell

* * *

Eight: A Discussion

Mountain guerilla post.
NANDO *and* MARCO. *They have rifles.*
MARCO *keeps watch.* NANDO *reads a book.*

MARCO: The allies are fighting Hitler at last – but Franco's safe. Democracies fight for their interests – not ideas. They live without ideas at home so why should they fight for them abroad?

NANDO (*looks up at the sky*): Fokkerschmidt. Reccy.

MARCO: He might see the tracks to the camp.

NANDO: Sheep.

MARCO: Too high for sheep.

> AGUSTINA *comes on left. She has a rifle.* NANDO *closes his book.*

AGUSTINA: He'll circle for hours.

> *They hide against the rock. After a while the plane's engine is heard.*

NANDO: They've rebuilt our village church. Big service to reopen it. One of the masons worked for us: he put a bomb inside the wall. Under a stone. Set in thin plaster so you could lift it out and time the bomb to go off in the service. Now it'll stay in its little niche till the church falls down.

MARCO: The mason was arrested. Police raided a café in town and he was at a meeting.

AGUSTINA: Cant someone else set it?

MARCO: Village full of police.

NANDO: Never get near it. Fascists believe only the brutal are capable of happiness. Once some of them trapped one of our comrades at the bottom of a cliff. He started to climb. They sprawled on the grass and smoked and jeered at him. Threw stones to dislodge the rubble onto his head. When he'd climbed sixty feet their officer shouted up 'Let's have some fun. If you fall we'll be satisfied. If you get to the top – we're down here'. He didn't believe them but he went on climbing. What else could he do? There were tears on his face. Sitting on the top – back where he couldnt see them – was another squad of Fascists. When he reached them they hauled him over the edge, took hold of his hands and feet and swung him in time to a Fascist tune. Then they threw him down to the others. When you hear of these things you realise we're all in danger. So you fight as naturally as you would if you were drowning. But you dont fight on your own. You have the strength of the others who're drowning. It makes each one of us as strong as a crowd. That's why we can fight against these odds.

The plane passes over them: noise and a shadow.

MARCO: After I buried Tomaso when he was shot in the hut I thought now I have to do the fighting of two men. Im not a coward. Thanks for the lesson. But we're throwing our lives away up here. Go back to the cities – live with the Fascists – attack from the inside. Up here I feel like a fly crawling over a tank.

AGUSTINA: You should mend your jacket. It looks shabby.

MARCO (*puts his arm through the rip in the flap of his jacket*): Brings me luck. Bayonet went through that. Im the unkillable soldier – both sides have tried.

AGUSTINA: I could get in the church. If they stopped me I'd say I'd heard the couple had been shot in my house so I thought I could move back – I didnt think anyone else would move in.

NANDO: They'd never believe you.

AGUSTINA: That doesnt matter as long as it sounds plausible. I wont carry a gun or anything suspicious and they wont know about the bomb. We could turn their celebration into a disaster. That's how their victories ought to be celebrated. If the bomb's there the rest is easy!

NANDO: What if they've found the bomb and are waiting for you?

AGUSTINA: That's a risk.

MARCO: She's the only one of us who's got an excuse to be there.

NANDO: How'd you get away? There'd be road blocks and patrols everywhere for the service.

AGUSTINA: I'd hide in our cellar.

NANDO: That's lunacy!

AGUSTINA: No – the house is empty now – if it isnt they'll all be in church. I'd have to hide somewhere quickly. And who'd think of looking there? I could hide for days and then come back through the hills.

MARCO: They might have found the cellar.

AGUSTINA: It would have been all over the papers. I can sleep under my own roof again – under my floor!

NANDO: I didnt go to my daughter's wedding. She's having a baby but I'll probably never see it. We've lost our home. We were apart for years. Now you've been here a few days and you're going away. War takes everything. I shant try to stop you. Be careful.

MARCO: When the gun sentry tried to describe you at his court martial they said you sounded like half the women in Spain. The factory girls are supposed to believe there are no shadows on your face – not even from your nose! And when you left the city it was night but a patch of daylight followed you so that you didnt bump into Police: a searchlight shining from the sky.

AGUSTINA: What use is a legend? People hear them and say: they're the big ones, we're ordinary. What do I want? A dry roof over my head and a warm blanket. Isnt that ordinary? And that no one blows up my world – that ought to be the most ordinary thing of all. People used to make revolutions to get bread – isnt it ordinary to want to eat? Now we have to make a revolution to stop them blowing the world to bits. We cant live with ignorance any more. We must fight everyone who stops us trying to understand ourselves. Today we have the power of god and so we must finally become human beings. To keep the ordinary things – the dry roof, bed, table – we must make a revolution. If we dont, everything will be blown to bits. Dont tell me about legends. The gun was there. My enemies walked in front of it. I fired. It was the most ordinary thing I've

ever done. I did it for the same reason I
lay the table or sweep the floor. If I'm a
legend my life is wasted.

   * * *

AGUSTINA:
It is my Spain!
Mine!
The fertile coasts and the rocky enduring
 heart are mine!
The red earth and apple orchards of
 Asturias
The cheese and butter pastures of
 Santander
The scallop road to Compostella
Are all mine!
Galicia where four sons each own part of
 one chicken
The desert below Madrid where the air is
 like a wolf's breath
The storm city of Toledo and its rapiers as
 deadly as lightning
The planes of La Mancha empty but for
 ghosts and the grim lakes
Estramadura raped by Latifundia
Andalusia where the sun comes to warm
 itself
And where olives, the fruit of poets, are
 grown
Cordoba the city of horses and silver
Sierra Nevada with its snows and sugar cane
Grenada where two rivers meet and the
 whole year is harvest
The rice fields of Valencia
The lost worlds of the Pyrenees where
 Hannibal's elephants left their bones
Monserrat the mountain of teeth and the
 holy grail
And where the earth lies like a giant on its
 back tearing at the sky
All these are mine!

In the mountains there are deer and goats
 and strangely swift boars
There are the eagles of Sierra de Cazola and
 the bone-breaker vulture
The storks that teach us fidelity
Scented deserts of thyme and tarragon
Roadsides thick with Prometheus' fennel
Bay and wattle
The rockrose from which came myrrh
The dark sweet myrtle and mandragora, the
 plant that shrieks
Pines and junipers and Spanish oaks
All mine!

It is a country of fools' churches and cretins'
 palaces
Where for each throne they built ten
 thousand cells
But all countries are like this

It is also a country of towns crowning hills
Of white walls as big as the paper giants
 write on
Of city pavements as graceful as crafted
 bowls
And everywhere steps and lanterns
There are the factories and mines of the
 north
The harbours at Cartegena
The Ramblas as wide and beautiful as the
 sea from which it rises
The chatter and laughter from darkened
 cafés
The frowning children at desks
And the two seas!
All these are mine
Who would not be happy in such a land?

   * * *

Nine: The Arrest

The house.
 AGUSTINA *comes on wearing her
knapsack.*

AGUSTINA:
I have been to the church
I counted the fissures
I inserted the blade into the plaster
I took out the stone
The wires grinned at me
I set the hands of the wristwatch to ten
And put back the stone

Now I return to the house that stands like a
 cairn of stones
In the field from which they were taken
When the house needed protecting in
 storms and frost
More stones were taken and new ones rose
 to take their place
The field bore stones in all seasons
It was its richest crop

New people live in my house
Curtains – our windows were bare –
And the door my husband left plain is
 painted
A bike leans on the wall
Signs that the house has prospered
I've stood here five minutes
If anyone was inside they'd have come to
 ask
Why I stand here

She goes into the house.

A proud housewife
Lace mats on the table
Rugs on the floor
By the sink military boots
The man is a civil guard
I go to the rug that covers the trapdoor to push it aside
And perhaps because there is so much new to see
And so much old to remember
I do not notice at first
Although it is light
That the whole floor is buried in six inches of concrete!

God! Not time to get in the hills! Troops – planes – all day to find me! O god . . . the bomb explodes in an hour. The shed! He's a civil guard! They might not even search here! (AGUSTINA *stands in the open doorway of the shed.*)

I watched the black smoke rush into the sky
Then heard the thud – as if it wished to make sure I knew the bomb had exploded
In the distance the voices sounded like children's
Cars hooted then silence
The smoke drifted over the village till it was a thin black veil draped in the sky.

AGUSTINA *goes into the shed – there is no door.* GUADALUPE *and* ROSITA *come on from right.*

ROSITA: They'll look for you.

GUADALUPE: For god's sake give it a rest! We must take them up to the hills! Drop them in a ditch! Cover it with old branches! They could have been there months. If they find them they're nothing to do with us – the whole village is as crooked as –

ROSITA: God you're a fool! They'll know it was you!

GUADALUPE: Its all we can do!

ROSITA: What if we're seen with them?

GUADALUPE: We wont be if we're quick!

ROSITA: You should never have taken them!

GUADALUPE *goes into the shed.*

GUADALUPE (*in the shed*): You wouldnt have come here if I hadnt! How could I afford what you expect on my salary?

ROSITA: I knew it'd be my fault!

GUADALUPE (*in the shed*): New curtains! New chairs! There's no end of it!

GUADALUPE *comes out of the shed with three petrol cans. He stands them by the door.*

Get the bike! (*He goes back into the shed.*) They wont miss a few cans of petrol. God knows what they waste driving their tarts round. Hurry. I've got to get back. I'll say I got knocked down in the stampede. Passed out. (*He comes out of the shed with three more petrol cans.*) Where's the bike? For god's sake dont stand there! Tie them on the bike or you'll need six journeys!

ROSITA *goes into the house.*
GUADALUPE *puts the cans next to the others.*

You're worth more than mother's milk. All goes well, I'll flog you in a few weeks.

GUADALUPE *goes back into the shed. After a few moments* AGUSTINA *comes out.* GUADALUPE *follows her pointing his gun.* ROSITA *comes from the house with the rope.*

ROSITA: Agustina – what is it?

GUADALUPE: Under the feed box. Tie her legs. You've got the rope. (ROSITA *ties* AGUSTINA*'s legs.*) Made a fine mess down there you sow.

AGUSTINA: What d'you mean? What happened? I heard the explosion. Why're you doing this?

GUADALUPE: Leave enough slack so she can walk. Pour it away and lose the cans. (ROSITA *finishes.*) Now walk, pig.

GUADALUPE *follows* AGUSTINA *out right.*

* * *

Chorus
You who are clothed and fed
Hear what the hungry have said
The hunger of the body is great
But the hunger of the mind is greater
The belly may be replete
But the sharp tooth of reason is not satisfied
You who sleep in bed with a pillow under your head
And dream the dreams of those who are fed

Remember what the hungry have said
Or you would be better off dead

* * *

Ten: The Soldier's Training

Mountains
  NANDO *comes on.*

NANDO: In five minutes I shall be dead. I cant kill myself. Not because of the pain. I cant end my mind.

  NANDO *takes a flag from his knapsack and drapes himself in it.* MANI *comes on with his* SOLDIERS.

MANI: Why?

NANDO: Our comrades were buried in it.

MANI: Bravo. (*To a* SOLDIER:) Pio you aim to miss when you're in the firing squad.

PIO (*unsure protest*): Sir.

MANI: I noticed. Dont worry, we're all cowards till we do something about it. (*Some of the* SOLDIERS *laugh.*) Shut up scum! You're not fit to fight with! Respect the boy! Here's a soldier who's afraid to kill. What use is he to you in a fight? Well scum? (*No response.*)

PIO: Sir –

MANI (*turns to* PIO): Dont speak. It will be like a conversion. Tomorrow you'll shave a different face. (*To the other soldiers.*) Sit. (*The soldiers sit cross legged.* MANI *kneels.*) Pio is going to do his first killing. (*To* NANDO:) If you want a priest I'll wait. (*No answer. To* PIO:) That flag is an insult. Lower it. (*To* NANDO:) Right hand – out. (NANDO *holds his right hand a foot away from his side.*) Out! (NANDO *lifts his right hand out at right angles. The flag hangs from his right hand and his shoulders.*) Aim at the right hand.

PIO *aims at* NANDO's *right hand.*

MANI: Breathe easily or you'll snatch at the trigger. Fire!

  A long pause. PIO *shoots. Misses.*

  Was that on purpose?

PIO: Sir.

MANI: Aim. (PIO *aims.*) Your rifle wont fire till its cocked.

CORPORAL: What a mess.

PIO *cocks his rifle and aims.*

MANI: Fire!

  A long pause. PIO *shoots. Hits. The end of the flag falls from* NANDO's *right hand. The hand bleeds.* NANDO *sways.*

NANDO: There is no god . . . god wouldnt let you breathe.

MANI: Its easy to drape yourself in a flag. Teach our simple Spanish soldier to endure with patience. Left hand. (NANDO *cant move.*) Look at the blue sky: so empty. The quartz shines in the rock. The smell of the dark pine wood below us. Even a running stream – and no fisherman's shadow on the water. God is good: he's given you all this and five minutes to enjoy it. I could have already shot you like a dog. We could be dropping your corpse over the cliff. Left hand.

NANDO *holds out his left hand, the flag hangs from it and his left shoulder.*

Fire!

  Shorter pause. PIO *fires. Hits. The flag falls to the ground. Both hands bleed.*

  (*To* CORPORAL:) Dont let him fall on the flag. (*The* CORPORAL *removes the flag.*) He's in a state of shock. He wont feel the wounds he dies of. You'd have thought he'd have felt them more than most wounded people. He doesnt feel any more than a potato does when you peel it. He cant even hear us now. Finish it off. (PIO *promptly cocks his rifle and aims.*) Fire!

PIO *fires immediately. Hits.* NANDO *falls dead.*

  (*Dangling his pistol in his hand.*) Good. that was the lesson: now the soldier fires on target to order.

PIO *marches to* MANI, *takes his pistol, marches to* NANDO *and shoots him in the head.*

  Amen.

MANI *gets to his feet and* PIO *marches to him. The other soldiers scramble up quickly.*

PIO (*returning pistol*): Pistol sir.

MANI: Long live death!

SOLDIERS: Long live death!

MANI: Christ the king!

SOLDIERS: Christ the king!

MANI: Throw him to the buzzards. (*To* PIO:) You'll make a good shot. A surprise.

PIO: Yessir.

SOLDIERS *take* NANDO *out right.* MANI *follows them.* SOLDIER 1 *and* PIO *are left.*

SOLDIER 1 (*offers* PIO *a cigarette*): All right? The boys'll have a whip round. Tonight we'll get you stinking drunk and carry you down to the whorehouse. You must have had a rough time these last weeks. Thats all over now. Tomorrow you'll be a new man.

PIO (*irritation, refusing the cigarette*): All right!

SOLDIER 1: Dont mind Jesus. First man he shot, he was drunk a week. You're better off with him than a lot of them.

PIO: Its all right – Im okay.

SOLDIER 1 (*lighting his own cigarette*): You're doing fine.

PIO *goes out right and* SOLDIER 1 *follows him.*

* * *

Song of Agustina Ruiz known as The Human Cannon

The fire will consume itself
The tempest will exhaust itself
The flood will return to the still deeps of the sea
But I will ride the world with my two talking horses
Till the generations of the earth are free

I do not ride in greed or scorn
I do not fight in rage or hate
Such passions as these are too brief and weak for me
But I will ride the world with my two talking horses
Till the generations of the earth are free

The seed that falls on stony ground
Shall turn the stones to fruitful earth
A garden will grow in the wastes of tyranny
And I will walk beside my two talking horses
As they gently bow their heads and graze the fields of liberty

For when the human will is weak
The laws of change shall still be strong
My womb and the earth shall give birth to liberty
And I will ride the world with my two talking horses
And you'll never never never conquer me

* * *

Eleven: Human Cannon

A town hall.

A large white room. On the right a desk, chairs and double doors to the street, on the left benches and a single door to the basement. The furniture and doors are dark oak.

The PRIEST *and* INVESTIGATOR *stand at a large arched window right. The* CLERK *sits at the desk and writes on forms.*

The INVESTIGATOR *is middle-aged, tall, big-chested, a bit flabby – sensual and intellectual.*

The civil guards wear uniform. The others in the room wear black.

INVESTIGATOR: I stopped my car on the road here to relieve myself. The middle of nowhere. Rocks and sand and a dead tree by an empty river. There were scraps of poster nailed to its trunk. Curled up like a dead animal. Unreadable. (*He picks up fragments from the desk. Reads*:) . . . 'When you use' something . . . (*To the* CLERK:) Find where it was printed.

PRIEST: They've taken hostages from the village. I suppose you know?

INVESTIGATOR: I asked for it to be done.

PRIEST: Ten. (*Half-question*:) It must be necessary . . . ?

INVESTIGATOR: I hope to let them go.

PRIEST: Its an ordeal.

INVESTIGATOR: They were kept overnight in a cell with Agustina Ruiz. Perhaps they've moved her to pity – though she must be made of stone. She denies placing the bomb. It would be better if she confessed. Then we'd be quite sure. Its not pleasant to think of a terrorist wandering round with another bomb. Confess or not she'll be shot. It should have been done before.

PRIEST: Local people respect her in spite of her politics.

INVESTIGATOR: All the more reason.

PRIEST: Why are the hostages women? Its made a bad impression.

INVESTIGATOR: Estarobon is a village of women. Most of the men died in the war. The Marquis cant lose any more labour. He has enough difficulties as it is.

The door, left, opens. CIVIL GUARDS *bring in* AGUSTINA *and ten other* WOMEN. BERTA TORBADO *is supported by one of the others. All the women are in black.*

GUARD: Against the wall.

PRIEST (*to the* INVESTIGATOR): Goodbye.

INVESTIGATOR: Stay.

PRIEST: It would be better –

INVESTIGATOR: You will reassure the innocent.

The women stand in a line against the wall, left.

It is not government policy to take hostages. All you women are suspects. (WOMEN *murmur in protest. He looks at a document.*) Gloria Vergara you were on the square the night before the bombing.

GLORIA VERGARA: I work at the Post Office. Its on the square.

INVESTIGATOR: Margarita Arrance you were on the square.

MARGARITA ARRANCE: I lost my cat. My neighbours will tell you. She was –

INVESTIGATOR: Renata Ortiz you were on the square. Seen by a Civil Guard, your nephew.

RENATA ORTIZ: I went to pray.

INVESTIGATOR: And so on. (*He lowers the document.*) Any of you could have entered the church when it was dark.

BERTA TORBADO (*timidly*): My mother's ill. Father ask them to let me go. I havent done anything wrong.

PRIEST: The neighbours are caring for her. You know Bertha . . . she doesnt really recognise you any more.

BERTA TORBADO: She might have another attack. They wont know what to do.

INVESTIGATOR: Father Roberto will visit her when he leaves.

NINA MIRAN: I was on the square. I go –

INVESTIGATOR: Your name?

NINA MIRAN: Nina Miran. I go every evening. My friend lives there. We've known each other since we were girls. Now she cant leave her house. We have a glass of wine together. Berta is sixty-nine. How could she get a bomb?

INVESTIGATOR: I dont think any of you did: it was Agustina Ruiz. The evidence is strong but circumstantial. I believe it satisfies justice. But it doesnt satisfy the army – nor should it. Justice can afford to make mistakes. Men are fallible but in time god corrects our errors. If the army fails no one corrects it. None of you should be in any doubt about what I say. If I cant be sure who committed this atrocity then everyone who could have committed it – you women – must be shot. You are a silent jury and the accused will pass the verdict – one way or the other – on you. Agustina Ruiz did you place the bomb in the church?

AGUSTINA: No.

INVESTIGATOR: Its coincidence you were hiding on the outskirts of the village just after the explosion?

AGUSTINA: I hoped to be allowed back in my house. After the shootings I didnt think anyone else would want to move in. When I heard the explosion I thought it was an air-raid so I hid.

INVESTIGATOR: You'd condemn these innocent women to death?

AGUSTINA: Who condemns them? They were on the square buying bread. Visiting friends. Going to church. It was their daily life. You arrest them. One is nearly seventy. Yes, father: last night they tortured people so that we could hear their screams. What sort of life d'you offer them anyway? Whenever you're goaded into frustration you drag them here off the street.

INVESTIGATOR (*to the other* WOMEN): I will give you a last chance to save yourself. The army will be satisfied with one witness to accuse her. If you tell me the truth you neednt stay in Estarobon. The Government will pay you the amount of a war widow's pension. (*He looks at the list.*) Teresa Martin. Who put the bomb in the church?

TERESA MARTIN: Yesterday my children washed and put on their best clothes and walked to the barracks. They didnt cry – they held hands. The whole town's talking about it. The soldiers must listen to them when they see their faces. They'll send a message to let me go. Dont make the children suffer.

INVESTIGATOR: Children have suffered. The Marquis Don Roberto Palmes De Serosan, Colonel Abrantes, Sister Anna and a farmer have been killed. Three children are among the wounded. One lost a leg. One will have a face hideous for life. And others may die. Who put the bomb in the church?

TERESA MARTIN: Estarobon.

INVESTIGATOR: No, who placed the bomb in the church?

TERESA MARTIN: Estarobon.

INVESTIGATOR: The village? The village placed the bomb? Nina Miran who placed the bomb in the church?

NINA MIRAN: Estarobon.

INVESTIGATOR: I see. And that is the answer of you all? Clerk put the question to the others and note their answers.

CLERK: Maria Barrios who placed the bomb in the church of Saint Vincent of Ferrer?

MARIA BARRIOS: Estarobon.

CLERK: Renata Ramones who placed the bomb in the church of Saint Vincent of Ferrer?

RENATA RAMONES: Estarobon.

CLERK: Maria Corves who placed the –

PRIEST: This is monstrous! Stop it! You dont know what you're doing! Why ever you were brought here, this is a crime! You could be shot! Berta I've taken the sacrament to your mother all the years she's been bedridden. I know you to be a devout christian. I ask you to tell the truth.

BERTA TORBADO: Father they say it was Estarobon. Estarobon.

INVESTIGATOR: Clerk, go on.

CLERK: Maria Corves who placed the bomb in the church of Saint Vincent of Ferrer?

MARIA CORVES: Estarobon.

CLERK: Gloria Vergara who placed the bomb in the church of Saint Vincent of Ferrer?

MANI *comes in through the doors, right, and sits at the desk.*

GLORIA VERGARA: Estarobon.

CLERK: Renata Ortiz who placed the bomb in the church of Saint Vincent of Ferrer?

RENATA ORTIZ: Estarobon.

CLERK: Junita Murciano who placed the bomb in the church of Saint Vincent of Ferrer?

JUNITA MURCIANO: Estarobon.

CLERK: Agustina Ruiz who placed the bomb in the church of Saint Vincent of Ferrer?

AGUSTINA: I dont know. I wasnt there.

PRIEST: What about the children in hospital?

AGUSTINA: The children in hospital. There are no more innocents. Not since you bombed cities. Where are the children of Guernica? For you a child is a thing you use as moral blackmail! We fight you for the sake of our children! Dont stand in your abbatoir and point your finger at me!

INVESTIGATOR: Let us turn to the murders of Private Albana and his wife.

AGUSTINA: I've already been cleared. I was on a train. Ask the military.

INVESTIGATOR: Where was your husband?

AGUSTINA: I dont know. I havent heard from him for a year.

INVESTIGATOR: He was hiding in the shed. He came out when it was dark and murdered the guard and his wife.

AGUSTINA: My husband wasnt there.

INVESTIGATOR: Where is he now?

AGUSTINA: Father Roberto thinks he may have got into France.

INVESTIGATOR: He's dead.

AGUSTINA (*pause. She shrugs her shoulders. Flatly, as if it ended the matter*): He's dead.

MANI: He kept us running for a whole day. No reason. He couldnt get away. By the time they caught him the soldiers were angry. So. (*He takes out a photo.*) Look at yourself. (*He gives the photo to* AGUSTINA.) From his jacket. There's some blood on the back.

TERESA MARTIN: He's the one who goes to the mountains in the lorry. They tell stories about him. I didnt believe it. Last night we said if we stick together they cant kill us, we're too many. Its not true! He'd kill us – and go on killing till there was no one left! And he (*She indicates the* INVESTIGATOR.) says Jose and Maria who were murdered –

GLORIA VERGARA: Teresa!

TERESA MARTIN: – she didnt tell us about that last night – we dont know what she's done! She put the bomb in the church. Agustina you told us last night.

INVESTIGATOR (*to the* CLERK): Teresa Martin. Strike her out. (*To* TERESA MARTIN:) Thank you. You have saved these women's lives. (*To the* GUARD:) Take her to the side. (*A* GUARD *takes* TERESA MARTIN *right, away from the other* WOMEN.) This defiance is now pointless. I have the witness I need. I ask you again: who put the bomb in the church?

SEVERAL WOMEN: Estarobon.

INVESTIGATOR: Estarobon is already infamous for its double murder and the bomb. Now this. I shall give an example to anyone else who is tempted to obstruct the Government when it seeks to protect its citizens. When Agustina Ruiz is shot, one of you women will be shot with her. (*To the* CLERK:) Pick a name.

CLERK (*confused*): How shall I –

INVESTIGATOR: Any name.

CLERK (*drops the list and picks it up, reads*): Nina Miran.

INVESTIGATOR (*to the* GUARD): Take her out.

A GUARD *starts taking* NINA MIRAN *out left.*

AGUSTINA: No!

INVESTIGATOR: You see what misery you cause! You've lost! The fanatics left in the mountains will turn their *friends* against them! *You* placed the bomb in the church!

AGUSTINA: No!

INVESTIGATOR: Look – bits of poster nailed up in the savanna. If you put them in the street they'd have been torn down before they were read! Who read it in the desert? The wind tore it up and threw it away! (*Reads fragments.*) . . . 'teach us' . . . 'teach us' . . .

AGUSTINA:
When you make us weak you teach us to be strong
When you use secret police you teach us to be secret
Its in our heads! You cant get rid of it!

AGUSTINA *moves towards the* INVESTIGATOR. *The* WOMEN *restrain her.* NINA MARTIN *turns back at the door.*

When you rob us you teach us to sabotage
When you exploit us you teach us to strike
When you make laws you teach us to break them

CIVIL GUARDS *move towards* AGUSTINA.

INVESTIGATOR (*to the* CIVIL GUARDS): Leave them.

AGUSTINA:
When you use weapons against us you teach us to arm
When Fascists imprison a country they teach it to be free!

As AGUSTINA *strains towards the* INVESTIGATOR, *the* WOMEN *hold her and her feet leave the ground so that her body becomes horizontal. The* WOMEN *stand round her like gunners limbering a gun. She raises her head to shout at the* INVESTIGATOR. *The* WOMEN *exclaim in astonishment.* AGUSTINA RUIZ *has become the human cannon.*

Destroy them! Their world! Cruel! Pull it down! Lift me higher! His head! Point me at his head! Head! Head! On him! Destroy him! My eyes. Smash! My mouth! Crush! Higher! Our world! Our hands! Our feet! The day! Up! Up! Doors open! Hear streets! Our world! Aim me! Head! Target! Higher! Now! Gun speaks! The bomb – who put – the church? It speaks! Not Estarobon! Fool! It was Spain! Spain!

The WOMEN *lower* AGUSTINA *to the ground.*

INVESTIGATOR: Open the doors. (*A* GUARD *opens the double doors, right.*) The eight may go.

The eight WOMEN *start to leave. A* GUARD *takes* NINA MIRAN *out left.*

Father, the nuns will give Teresa Martin a room for the time being. Put her children in a home till the village is quiet. (*The* PRIEST *nods.*)

MANI: Excellency.

MANI *goes out right.*

INVESTIGATOR (*to the* PRIEST): Go to that woman.

PRIEST: When she's ready. Let her grieve first.

WOMEN (*turning at the door, to* AGUSTINA): Goodbye. We didnt disgrace ourselves. We'll tell the village about you.

The WOMEN *go.*

TERESA MARTIN (*to* AGUSTINA): My children are so little. I tried to give them a good life. It was so hard. They'd have taken them away and beaten them for having a wicked mother. I cant let anyone hurt my children.

AGUSTINA: It doesnt matter.

The PRIEST *and* TERESA MARTIN *go out right. Two* GUARDS *are left. One shuts the double doors. The other places a chair for* AGUSTINA *to sit on. She stands.*

INVESTIGATOR: Our era has begun. Fascism is normality protected from change. Most people will hardly notice. The streets will be cleaner. There'll be no strikes. And people like you will have vanished. The world you want is a Utopia. I can see your pathetic army setting out for the horizon, each one bowed under the weight of his brick. When they began to fall you'd turn on them with your whips. You'd feel justified, after all you're leading them to paradise. Soon they'd run berserk and you'd have a world of brutes. Life is short. They want to enjoy it. We'll give them food and holidays – and festivals where they can thank their protectors. They'll be content, and that is paradise. What sort of a woman shrugs when she's told her husband is dead? – In paradise the flowers are brighter. Most people wont notice it. To do that you have to bear the misery of journeying to the horizon – and we'll do that for them. They wont know the brightness of paradise – but they'll be spared being brought face to face with their own littleness. Which is hell. That's all you offered them. That's why we get rid of you.

* * *

Chorus
Year after year the workers toiled
And plowmen bowed their heads to the
 ground
Till they were driven to die in war
But the lives they lived have made us strong
And to our children we pass our strength
The fruit they eat will ripen in light
And with joy we eat the bitter fruit
That ripened in the night

* * *

Twelve: The Smile

Mountain Road.
 AGUSTINA, NINA MIRAN, GUARDS 1 *and* 2.
NINA MIRAN *makes a gesture to take* AGUSTINA's *arm.*

GUARD 1: Prisoners cant touch.

NINA MIRAN (*moving away*): Poor child its easier for me. Forgive me. I sat at home all day till it was time to go to my friend for our evening glass. My life was already over. How many died from our village? Perhaps now the suffering can end sooner.

TINA *comes on left with her baby in her arms.*

GUARD 2 (*to* TINA): Hurry its just starting.

TINA (*shouts, holding out the child*): Mother.

AGUSTINA (*shouts*): Thank you!

TINA: I went to town. They said here. No lift. Ran. (*She looks down at the child.*) All right now. Hold it.

GUARD 1: Prisoners cant touch.

AGUSTINA: Mine.

TINA (*takes a few steps towards* AGUSTINA): Please.

CORPORAL (*off*): Ready!

    GUARD 1 *starts to take* AGUSTINA *left.*

AGUSTINA (*bewildered*): What?

NINA MIRAN: Take me first.

GUARD 1 (*papers*): You're down second. All right, say I got it wrong.

    GUARD 1 *takes* NINA MIRAN *out left.*

AGUSTINA: Her face. The shawl. (TINA *lifts the shawl.*)

    CORPORAL *comes on left.*

CORPORAL: What's going on?

GUARD 2: Civilian talking to prisoner corp.

TINA (*giving the child to* GUARD 2): Give it to her.

GUARD 2 (*looks down at the baby in his arms*): What?

CORPORAL (*panic*): Search it! The shawl!

GUARD 2 (*panic*): What is – is it? – (*He pulls at the child's clothes as if they were burning.*)

TINA: Careful!

CORPORAL (*panic*): Pistol! Grenade!

GUARD 2 (*panic, throws the shawl to the* CORPORAL): Empty!

CORPORAL (*panic*): Nappy! Vest! The back!

    GUARD 2 *searches the baby. The* CORPORAL *holds the shawl out like a magician's square: turns it round to show its empty both sides. Off, a burst of machine-gun fire. It rattles on the rocks.* Not to be trusted.

GUARD 2 (*finishes searching*): Nothing.

CORPORAL: All right let her look.

    GUARD 2 *holds the baby up in front of* AGUSTINA *for her to see.* AGUSTINA *makes a slight step towards the baby.*

Stay!

AGUSTINA (*looking at the child*): Its father . . . ?

TINA: I dont know.

AGUSTINA: He'll be safe. You came. So far. I'm glad. Dont cry. It doesnt help. (*She smiles at the child.*) There: all these years from now it will remember me smiling.

    Off, a single shot. AGUSTINA *doesnt take her eyes of the child.*

(*Smiling:*) She doesn't mind the shooting. You'd better go.

TINA *takes the child from* GUARD 2 *and starts to leave.*

(*Smiling:*) Her face.

TINA *hurries right, turns the child on her shoulder so that it faces back to* AGUSTINA.

(*Smiling:*) Higher.

TINA *lifts the child higher.* GUARD 1 *comes on.*

(*Gesturing to the* SOLDIERS *to wait. Smiling:*) A little longer.

TINA *goes out right with the child.* AGUSTINA *stops smiling and turns to the* SOLDIERS. *She goes out with them.*